EARTH, WIND, FIRE, AND RAIN

TRUE STORIES

Real Tales of Temperamental Elements

JUDY DODGE CUMMINGS

Nomad Press
A division of Nomad Communications
10 9 8 7 6 5 4 3 2 1

This book was manufactured by CGB Printers,
North Mankato, Minnesota, United States
February 2018, Job # 240589
ISBN Softcover: 978-1-61930-628-8
ISBN Hardcover: 978-1-61930-626-4

Educational Consultant, Marla Conn

Questions regarding the ordering of this book should be addressed to
Nomad Press
2456 Christian St.
White River Junction, VT 05001
www.nomadpress.net

Printed in the United States.

Contents

Titles in the **Mystery & Mayhem** Series

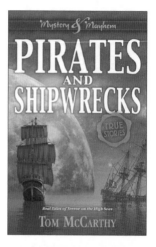

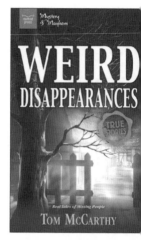

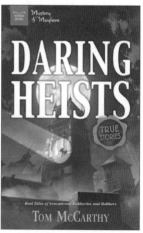

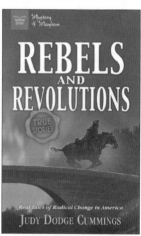

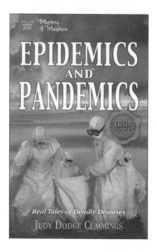

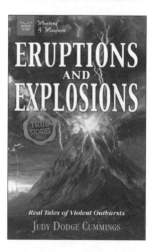

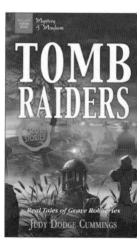

Check out more titles at www.nomadpress.net

Introduction

When Disaster Strikes

Earth, wind, fire, and water—the ancient
Greeks believed these four elements were the
foundation of life. Earth provides nourishment,
wind is the air we breathe, fire warms and
lights, and water cleanses and quenches.

But nature is fickle. While these elements give life,
they also take it away.

The power of a natural disaster is chilling. The
blue sky, calm water, and solid ground we take for
granted can turn on us with sudden fury. When
nature gets ugly, it is a stark reminder that no matter
how advanced civilization becomes, we will always
be at the mercy of the elements.

Five of America's deadliest natural disasters were
made worse by human error, ignorance, and greed.

Earth, Wind, Fire, and Rain

In 1871, the vast forest of northern Wisconsin was a tinderbox. While loggers, railroad workers, and farmers in the town of Peshtigo prayed for rain, they kept chopping down trees and burning brush. On October 8, small blazes joined hands in a funnel of flame that burned 1 million acres of forest in the deadliest fire in American history.

The people in Peshtigo knew fire posed a threat during that dry summer, but the residents of New York City were blindsided by the "Great White Hurricane" that hit on March 11, 1888. Meteorologists had predicted clearing skies, but then two storm fronts collided, bringing New York City to its knees.

Communication with the outside world was cut off and all transportation ground to a halt. People froze to death in snowdrifts more than 10 feet high. Others drowned in the icy harbor.

Powerless, too, were the residents of Johnstown, Pennsylvania, on May 31, 1889. A private club of wealthy businessmen owned a dam upriver from Johnstown. The club modified the dam to improve recreation on its private lake, but these changes weakened the structure. When heavy rains fell, the dam burst, sending 20 million tons of water downriver.

Although the dam was clearly the creation of man, the courts deemed the flood an act of God. No one was held responsible for the destruction.

When Disaster Strikes

Of course, no one is at fault when an earthquake strikes. On April 18, 1906, the ground under San Francisco, California, began to shake and crack. A massive earthquake toppled buildings and broke water and gas mains. Fires erupted across the city that could not be blamed on nature alone. Years of corruption and mismanagement by officials left the fire department unprepared to battle the blazes. For three days, San Francisco burned.

Drought and strong winds were common to the Southern Plains, but in the 1920s, farmers replaced the natural grasses that held the soil in place with millions of acres of wheat. Nature got even by transforming this breadbasket into the Dust Bowl. On April 14, 1935, winds from Canada moved across the flat land at speeds of 65 miles an hour, picking up soil as it blew. A cloud of dirt stretched 200 miles wide, suffocating livestock, smothering crops, and burying houses and people in dirt. "Black Sunday" was just the beginning of an ecological nightmare.

These natural disasters cost millions of dollars and caused much death and misery. But they also sparked reforms that changed America. Fire prevention strategies, disaster response plans, and improvements in weather forecasting, architecture, and agriculture developed after the clouds passed and the fires were put out. These advances save lives.

But remember—no one controls nature. Be prepared to get out of the way when disaster strikes.

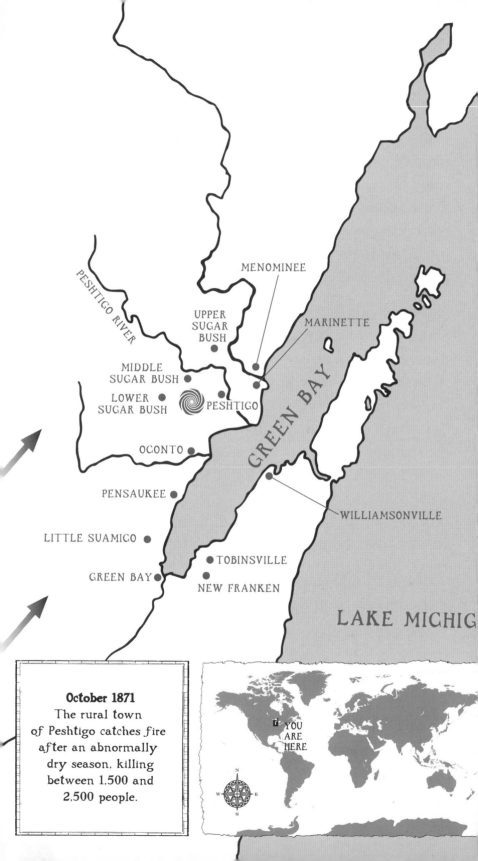

MENOMINEE

PESHTIGO RIVER

UPPER
SUGAR
BUSH

MARINETTE

MIDDLE
SUGAR BUSH

LOWER
SUGAR BUSH

PESHTIGO

GREEN BAY

OCONTO

PENSAUKEE

WILLIAMSONVILLE

LITTLE SUAMICO

TOBINSVILLE

GREEN BAY

NEW FRANKEN

LAKE MICHIG

October 1871
The rural town
of Peshtigo catches fire
after an abnormally
dry season, killing
between 1,500 and
2,500 people.

YOU
ARE
HERE

N
W — E
S

1865
he American
vil War ends

1871
The Peshtigo Fire
burns the town

1881
Clara Barton
creates the Red
Cross, which
comes to the aid
of those suffering
during a disaster

Chapter One

Eden Burning

Long ago in northeast Wisconsin, a forest grew.
Hundreds and thousands of acres of hemlock,
oak, maple, and pine trees stood shoulder to
shoulder. Catholic priest Peter Pernin came to
the area in 1870 and described it as "a wild
but majestic forest. Trees, trees, everywhere,
nothing else but trees as far as you can travel."
The king of the forest was the white pine.

Six feet wide and 170 feet tall, just one tree could be
used to complete an entire house. To lumbermen,
these pines were gold. The wild and rapid Peshtigo
River cut a crooked path through the forest, and by
the mid 1800s, sawmills had sprung up along its
banks.

At the sawmills, logs were cut into boards to be sent downriver to the Green Bay of Lake Michigan. From there, the timber was shipped to Chicago, 250 miles south.

Farmers followed the loggers north, and the little town of Peshtigo was born. A journalist from Detroit, Michigan, was taken by its beauty. "Wisconsin is the Eden of our country," he wrote.

But this paradise would be short-lived. On October 8, 1871, drought, human carelessness, and combustible weather ignited the deadliest fire in American history. Eden burned.

———◆———

When Father Pernin arrived in 1870, the town of Peshtigo was booming. Chicago businessman William Ogden founded the Peshtigo Company in 1856. The company included a sawmill, woodenware factory, dry-goods store, and boardinghouse. A harbor into Green Bay lay only 6 miles southeast of town, so lumber could be shipped south across Lake Michigan.

However, travel on the Great Lakes could be treacherous. In 1864, Ogden decided to create an alternative, and partnered with lumberman Isaac Stephenson to extend the Chicago Northwestern railroad from the city of Green Bay to the Menominee River, 10 miles north of Peshtigo. Hundreds of laborers moved north to lay the tracks.

Peshtigo was home to roughly 2,000 people. The river cut the town in half, with the two sides connected by a wooden bridge. Immigrant farmers from Sweden, Germany, and Norway bumped elbows with loggers and railroad workers on sawdust streets and plank sidewalks.

Women shopped at F.J. Bartels dry goods or J.J. Sherman's drugstore. A curtain factory and gristmill provided locals with more jobs, while two hotels sheltered visitors.

On Saturday nights, the logging and railroad crews relaxed at Peshtigo's dozens of saloons. Sunday mornings, citizens could seek forgiveness at Father Pernin's almost-completed Catholic church, St. Mary's. By October 1871, the building was almost finished. The final task of plastering the walls was scheduled for October 9.

Father Pernin would never get to preach in the new building.

———◆———

Not everyone lived in the town of Peshtigo. West of town, the Sugar Bush was a collection of farm settlements sheltered by a heavy stand of sugar maples. North of Peshtigo were the towns of Marinette and Menominee.

Earth, Wind, Fire, and Rain

Fire enabled people to make a living from the land. Fire was used to clear fields, dispose of brush and debris, cook food, heat houses, power train engines, and fuel sawmill boilers. Occasionally, a fire would get out of hand and burn a few acres. But in normal times, fires died out quickly in the moist, windless, dark forest.

The fall of 1871 was not a normal time.

Every winter, northern Wisconsin was blanketed in several feet of snow. During the winter of 1871, no snow fell. Springs rains were light and ended early. After July 16, it was as if a spigot in the sky had been cranked closed. Except for a light sprinkle on September 16, no rain fell.

The land became parched. Miles of swamp and cranberry bog dried up. The Peshtigo River sank so low, logs could not be floated downriver. Instead, they were piled along the bank. Leaves and pine needles died and fell, blanketing the forest floor.

Despite the dryness, life continued on for the locals. Farmers burned off stumps to clear the fields. Hunters scoured the woods for game and their spent ammunition fell, still smoldering, to the forest floor. Sparks from locomotive brake lines and smokestacks fell in the dry brush along the train tracks. Flammable industrial chemicals were used at the mills.

In this tinderbox, small fires did not die. They went dormant. Sparks nibbled at tree roots or hid in stumps. Coals smoldered inside peat bogs. People traveling at night reported tiny red eyes glaring out from the woods. It was fire.

Peshtigo had no fire department. Instead, one single-pump fire engine was parked at William Ogden's sawmill. Barrels of water were stationed around town, and everyone kept a bucket handy. When the lumber company's whistle blew or the church bells rang, people grabbed their buckets and headed toward the smoke.

This system of firefighting worked for small fires, but would prove useless on October 8, 1871. Conditions were ripe for a fire of epic proportions.

A low-pressure weather system moved in from the Plains at the end of September. When there is low pressure over a region, the atmosphere pushes more lightly on the earth in that spot than it does in the surrounding area. This light pressure allows the air to rise in a kind of atmospheric valley. Outside air rushes in to replace the rising air, creating a counterclockwise spin.

When the low-pressure system covers a large area, the spinning air creates very powerful winds.

Wind and fire are a deadly combination.

The air around Peshtigo was bone dry, just what fire needs to thrive. When a fire burns, the hot air around the flame rises in a pillar of gas, smoke, and debris called a convection column. As cool air flows in to take the place of the rising hot air, the fresh oxygen feeds the flame. Then, that cool air heats up and also rises, shooting the convection column even higher.

Sometimes, a fire's heat becomes so intense, it creates its own wind system. The heat sends an updraft of wind shooting up and sucks in surrounding air, creating fierce winds that blow toward the center of the fire. This is what is known as a firestorm.

Firestorms are devilishly hot, large, and fast. Their temperatures can reach 2,000 degrees and have been known to cover land the size of 33 football fields.

When wind pushes fire across flat land and slams into wind hiding behind a land ridge or stand of trees, the two airstreams join hands and spin, forming fire whirls or fire tornadoes. Fire whirls rotate at speeds of 22 to 67 miles per hour and range in size from 1 to 500 feet wide.

Worse are the fire tornadoes. These twisters can be 1,000 feet around and rotate at 110 miles an hour.

A firestorm is ravenous. It will consume hay, bark, kerosene, sawdust, buildings, leaves, and flesh.

Eden Burning

The residents of Peshtigo would soon discover that a firestorm will not stop until everything in its path has been devoured.

———◆———

The residents of Peshtigo received warnings that a catastrophe was looming. On September 16, the *Peshtigo Eagle* newspaper reported, "Heavy fires on the east of the village in the woods." Smoke was thick and the air tasted of burnt sugar and grit. On September 21, the sawmill at Oconto, a community south of Peshtigo, caught fire. Before it was extinguished, the fire gnawed through the telegraph lines between Green Bay and Marinette.

Peshtigo was now cut off from the outside world.

Father Pernin ventured to Sugar Bush on September 22 to visit some families from his congregation. At the last farm he visited, a 12-year-old boy offered to take Pernin pheasant hunting. The two spent a few enjoyable hours in the forest, and when the sun began to set, Pernin asked the lad to guide them back to the farm.

After 30 minutes of wandering, the boy admitted he was lost. Darkness and silence descended on the forest.

Beneath the quiet, Pernin heard "the crackling of tiny fire that ran along the ground . . . among the trunks of the trees, leaving them unscathed but devouring the dry leaves." Pernin looked up. The tree tops swayed in the rising wind.

They were in danger.

Pernin and the boy shouted for help. Finally, the boy's family heard their cries. As if sensing its prey was about to escape, the fire flared up and formed a circle around the lost pair, cutting them off from the rescue party. The rescuers used heavy branches to beat down the flames in a narrow path. Pernin and the boy managed to escape the circle of death.

Little fires like this were erupting everywhere. On September 23, barns, livestock, fences, and houses suddenly ignited in communities around Peshtigo. These fires were doused, but the frisky winds tossed sparks across the Peshtigo River, lighting the sawdust and slabs that lay next to the woodenware factory.

A bucket brigade put the flames out, but peoples' nerves grew frayed as rain still did not fall.

The following morning, every pew was full in all three of Peshtigo's churches as townsfolk prayed for rain. As if to tease the worshippers, a fire whistle blew in the middle of services. The sawdust near the woodenware factory was ablaze again. Winds were stirring up small fires in the woods across the river.

The town spent that Sunday fighting the fires. Father Pernin described how flames wound "about [the tallest trees] like a huge serpent. . . . Hissing and glaring . . . its fierce breath swept off the green leaves." Thousands of birds soared into the air to escape the heat of the burning trees. They hovered briefly before being sucked back into the inferno.

By evening, the winds died down and the fires did, too. The next morning, winds chased away the clouds of smoke, and people breathed a sigh of relief. The immediate crisis seemed over.

This close call did not scare the people of Peshtigo into making dramatic changes. Work at the sawmill and woodenware factory was stopped on Monday, September 25, but after that, people relaxed their guard. The trees around town were blackened, so everyone assumed they could not catch on fire again.

Like his neighbors, Father Pernin admitted that he did not feel "any great anxiety" about the weather. He should have.

———◆———

The morning of Saturday, October 7, winds blew from the southwest, growing stronger as the day wore on. At 4 in the afternoon, a steamboat docked at Peshtigo Harbor, depositing 100 Scandinavian immigrants on shore.

These people had come to Wisconsin in search of paradise, but when they stepped off the boat, they must have wondered what kind of Eden this was. A blizzard of ash and sand fell so thickly that they could see only about 12 feet in front of them.

Sunday, October 8, was a chilly morning. The gritty smoke in the air made it hard to breath. Townsfolk eyed local animals nervously. Cats scrambled down the sidewalk in packs. Deer stumbled out on the road and dogs crowded meekly near their hooves.

Father Pernin understood how the animals felt. He woke with a sense of "impending calamity."

At 7 in the evening, the priest went to check on a neighborhood widow. As they chatted in the woman's yard, a tree spontaneously burst into flames. "It was just as if the wind were a breath of fire," Pernin recalled. They put the fire out, but Pernin's anxiety was not so easily quenched.

The priest returned to his house and grabbed a shovel. He began to dig a large trench in his yard. The sandy soil was light, but the work was hard because the smoky air burned his throat every time he inhaled. Still, fear kept Pernin digging.

A bank of crimson clouds in the western sky grew larger. Between each thud of his shovel, Pernin heard a "strange and terrible" noise that sounded like a "locomotive . . . or the rumbling of thunder."

The sound gave the priest what he later described as "supernatural strength." When he finished digging,

Pernin ran into his house. A few minutes later, he came out dragging a heavy trunk full of his clothing and personal items.

Pernin was burying his trunk when his next-door neighbor came outside. "Father," she asked. "Do you think there is any danger?"

Pernin confessed that he suspected things were going to get very bad.

"But if a fire breaks out, what are we to do?" asked the woman.

"Seek the river at once," he replied. A few minutes later, the woman and her family ran for the river. The wind gusted, almost lifting Pernin from his feet. Now the roar sounded as though it was almost overhead. Father Pernin shook himself. What was he waiting for? He needed to get to the river, too!

Suddenly, the priest remembered the Eucharist, the holy bread and wine he served during Mass. The Eucharist is considered sacred by Catholics who believe this bread and wine is the body and blood of Jesus, their savior.

Pernin kept the holy bread in a small wooden box called a tabernacle. When the church was emptied to prepare it for plastering, the priest had moved the tabernacle to his house.

Now he dashed inside and took the box from the closet. Pernin tried to insert a key into the tiny keyhole, but his hand shook. The key fell to the ground. Outside the wind bellowed in anger. He did not have time to hunt for the key, so Pernin just carried the entire tabernacle outside. He set the box in his wagon and darted back into the house to get the wine chalice.

Inside, the air was dry as bone. He grabbed the chalice and ran back out. As soon as he stepped outside, Pernin knew he should have headed for the river earlier.

The wind slammed him to the ground. Pernin rose, legs trembling with the effort of resisting the powerful gusts. The wind yanked on the wagon, trying to steal it from Pernin's grip, but the priest refused to let go. He grabbed his garden gate with his other hand, but the wind snatched it away, hurling the gate into the sky along with the garden fence.

Every breath Pernin inhaled felt like he was swallowing a lit match. He closed his eyes against the onslaught of cinders, sand, and smoke.

As Pernin made his way blindly toward the river, a terrifying din filled his ears. Horses screaming. Bricks cracking. Trees crashing. Bodies thudding. Louder than anything else were the angry bellow of the wind and the ravenous crackle of the fire.

Pernin reached the river and saw flames skim across the water as if it was a field of grass. People from both sides of town crowded onto the bridge. Pernin did not join them. Under the weight of the terrified stampede of people and animals, he knew the bridge was bound to collapse.

At a section where the river dropped off quickly, Pernin pushed his wagon into the water as deeply as he could. He prayed the tabernacle would be safe, and then concentrated on saving himself. Pernin waded out up to his neck. He scanned the river bank. Many people stood at the water's edge just staring up at the swirling cloud of fire.

It was as if they had resigned themselves to death.

It was 10 p.m. when Pernin entered the river, and the night lasted an eternity. For hours, he fought to breathe the scalding air and keep his head from catching fire. Hands constantly in motion, Pernin splashed water on his face and beat back flames as he witnessed life-and-death struggles around him.

One woman arrived at the riverbank clutching a bundle to her chest. When she opened the blanket, anguish twisted her face.

"Ah! My child!" she cried. The bundle was empty. In her flight to the river, the woman's baby must have slipped from her arms. Later that night, the woman drowned herself.

The bridge did eventually collapse, tossing people and their belongings into the strong current. Those who did not burn, drowned.

One woman kept afloat by hanging onto a log. A cow bumped into her and knocked her off the log. The woman sank and Pernin assumed she had drowned. A little later, the woman drifted by again, one hand latched tightly to the cow's horns. Both the woman and the cow survived the night.

Even with the fire raging overhead, the waters of the Peshtigo River were cold. It was October in northern Wisconsin, after all. People began to shiver and tremble. But still the heavens blazed and no one dared leave the river. A woman standing near Pernin for hours finally spoke.

"Do you not think this is the end of the world?" she asked.

"I do not think so," Pernin replied. "But if other countries are burned as ours . . . the end of the world . . . must be at hand."

◆

The world did not end, but Peshtigo would never be the same. Around 3:30 in the morning, the fire died down enough so Pernin thought it was safe to leave the river. He crawled up on the bank, removed his outer clothes, and lay on the warm sand to chase the chill from his waterlogged bones.

After a brief rest, Pernin tried to rise. He could not. His chest was heavy and each inhalation was like trying to breathe through a straw. His throat was so swollen he could not speak. Most painful were Pernin's scalded, sand-scratched eyes.

Someone guided the priest to a sheltered valley along the riverbank that the flames had skipped over. While Pernin and other injured people curled up in the sand, the uninjured searched for loved ones.

They returned with a horror story. All that remained of Peshtigo was debris and charred corpses.

That night, the heavens opened and it rained.

Hundreds of injured, including Pernin, were transported to Marinette, but this small community could not care for them all. Telegraph lines were still down, so a steamboat captain carried a plea for help to the city of Green Bay.

Authorities there telegraphed a message to Governor Lucius Fairchild's office in Madison. But the governor was out of town. Chicago, too, had caught fire on October 8, hammered by the same wild winds as Peshtigo. Governor Fairchild had gone south to aid that city.

The governor's 24-year-old wife, Francis Fairchild, took charge of relief efforts. When she learned a train loaded with relief supplies was ready to depart for Chicago, she sent it to Peshtigo instead. It provided blankets, clothing, wagons, and food to the devastated people of Peshtigo.

But the death toll still rose.

The treatment for burns in 1871 included only salves and bandages. Many burn victims died within hours from kidney failure. Some survivors in remote areas starved to death because aid did not reach them quickly enough. There was no food to be found in the fire-ravaged land. Other people died from infections when gangrene set into their deep burns.

Father Pernin returned to Peshtigo on October 11 to help bury the dead. He later wrote, "No pen could fully describe nor words do justice," to what he saw. All that remained of the town were blackened tree trunks, the boilers of two train engines, the twisted iron of wagon wheels, and the stone foundation of the woodenware factory.

The land was "a desert recalling a field of battle."

Charred horses, cows, and people sprawled everywhere. Lucky were those survivors who were able to identify their dead loved ones from a ring or belt buckle. Many people had been reduced to ash.

There were 70 dead bodies in the boardinghouse. Twenty people had stuffed themselves inside a well. The fire had soared over them, but they had all suffocated.

The bodies of a man and his two children were found with their throats slit. This father had decided that this was a kinder fate for his children than burning to death.

All that remained of St. Mary's was the church bell. One half of the bell was intact, but the other half had melted. Near the ash that had once been his house, Pernin dug up his buried trunk. Except for a burned handle, it was unscathed, and the clothing inside appeared to be in perfect condition. But when Pernin picked up a piece of cloth, it crumbled in his hands.

The priest had lost everything.

Heartsick, Father Pernin walked across the charred beams that were all that remained of the town's bridge. On the other side of the river a member of his church saw him and cried, "Come quickly . . . it is a great miracle!"

Pernin was led to the place where he had shoved his wagon into the river. The wagon had toppled over and been badly burned. But when the wagon fell, the tabernacle was tossed on top of a log. There it still remained, unharmed.

The survival of this sacred box lifted Pernin's spirits. He left the tabernacle on the log for two days so people could view it and feel stronger. Then he returned to Marinette, bringing the tabernacle with him. When Father Pernin pried open the lock, the holy bread was still inside and undamaged.

The fire destroyed 1.5 million dollars worth of William Ogden's property. He had a fortune to recoup and northern Wisconsin still had a lot of trees. On October 14, Ogden announced, "We will rebuild this village . . . ." He kept his promise, but Peshtigo had lost its momentum.

The sawmill and harbor were rebuilt, but not the woodenware factory. This loss cost the town many jobs. As the railroad expanded farther north, businessmen moved their investments from the logging industry to the iron mines of Michigan. Peshtigo became just another small Wisconsin town.

Chicago's fire stole the limelight that terrible day.

Eden Burning

No one outside northeast Wisconsin learned of Peshtigo's inferno until later. In contrast, reporters flocked to Chicago. They fed the nation's appetite for gore and misery, and even took photographs.

The residents of Peshtigo were too busy trying to stay alive to capture the firestorm on camera.

According to the Wisconsin Historical Society, 1,152 people in and around Peshtigo were confirmed dead after the fire and another 350 were presumed to have perished. In addition, 1,500 people were seriously injured and 3,000 left homeless.

Entire families were incinerated as Eden burned.

Eventually, trees regrew in America's Eden, covering the scarred land. But the town of Peshtigo, Wisconsin, has not forgotten what happened on October 8, 1871. The city has a fire museum that details the disaster. Beside the museum is a small cemetery with a mass grave that holds the ashes of 350 unidentified victims. This is a gruesome reminder of what happens when humans push nature too far and nature pushes back. But some hope also lies in Peshtigo's tragic story. The museum features a special display—Father Pernin's tabernacle.

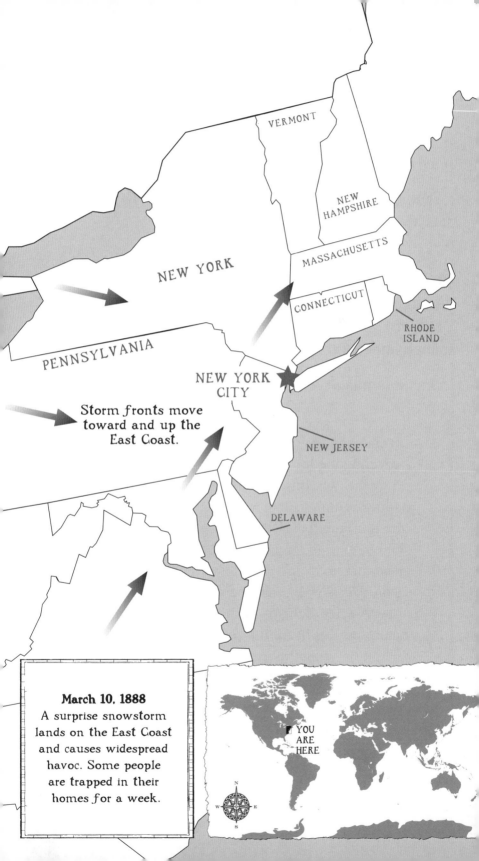

VERMONT

NEW HAMPSHIRE

NEW YORK

MASSACHUSETTS

CONNECTICUT

RHODE ISLAND

PENNSYLVANIA

NEW YORK CITY

Storm fronts move toward and up the East Coast.

NEW JERSEY

DELAWARE

March 10, 1888
A surprise snowstorm lands on the East Coast and causes widespread havoc. Some people are trapped in their homes for a week.

YOU ARE HERE

N
W   E
S

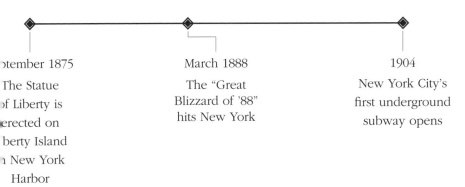

>tember 1875
The Statue
>f Liberty is
erected on
berty Island
า New York
Harbor

March 1888
The "Great
Blizzard of '88"
hits New York

1904
New York City's
first underground
subway opens

Chapter Two

Great White Hurricane

When spring sauntered into the northeastern
United States in March 1888, looking like
she intended to stay, everyone assumed Old
Man Winter had left town. The temperature
was a balmy 50 degrees Fahrenheit (10
degrees Celsius). Robins strutted on lawns
dotted with purple and yellow crocuses.
The sunshine beckoned people outdoors.

In Buffalo, New York, 17-year-old Sara Wilson bought
a new spring hat with a long, red feather. Other
children begged to go see the circus, including
10-year-old Sam Strong, an orphan who lived in New
York City with his aunt and uncle.

While everyone was gawking at spring, Old Man Winter prepared for one final blow of the season. His punch, the "Great Blizzard of '88," would paralyze New York City for days and reveal serious flaws in urban America.

In 1888, New York was a city in motion. Surrounded by water, it had one of the busiest ports in the world. Ferry boats transported commuters across the Hudson and East Rivers to jobs in Manhattan. The Statue of Liberty, only recently opened to the public, loomed in the bay. The water around it was dotted with sailing ships, fishing schooners, steamers, and yachts.

Lower Manhattan was the hub of the city's economy. The markets, offices, hotels, and docks teemed with people.

To navigate the sidewalk, pedestrians had to step around newspaper stalls, shoeshine stands, and peddlers bartering with old women. Children raced by on roller skates, zipping past overflowing garbage cans. New York did not have regular trash collectors, so garbage usually rotted for days.

The streets were also always in shadow, even on the beautiful day of Saturday, March 10, 1888.

photo credit: Detroit Publishing Co.

The web of telegraph, telephone, and electric wires dangling from utility poles was so thick it blocked out sunlight.

Pedestrians needed to be on guard when crossing the streets. Horse-drawn cabs, carriages, and wagons were everywhere. Sometimes, the rumble of an elevated train, or el train, on one of the four iron trestles that ran above the city spooked a horse into running. About 50,000 New Yorkers depended on these el trains for their daily commute.

Commuters relied on the daily forecasts of the U.S. Weather Service to let them know how long their ride to work would take.

Created by Congress in 1870, the U.S. Weather Service was originally run by the military and was headquartered in Washington, DC. Three times a day, six days a week, workers at 154 substations across the country telegraphed weather data to Washington for meteorologists to analyze. Then, headquarters sent each station a regional weather report.

The substation for New York City was located in the Equitable Assurance Building on Broadway Avenue. The only time this station closed was between 10 p.m. on Saturdays and 5 p.m. on Sundays.

Tourists often visited the building, riding the newfangled hydraulic elevators to the top floor and walking out on the roof. There, visitors could watch the weathermen in action as they collected data from their instruments. The anemometer, which measured wind speed, was attached to the roof's tower, 172 feet above the ground.

The morning of March 10, Washington meteorologists notified Sergeant Elias Dunn, the chief of the New York weather station, that two storm systems were headed his way.

A low-pressure front was moving through the Midwest, bringing snow to Minnesota and a tornado in Wisconsin. That storm was moving 600 miles per day. A second weather front of warm, wet air was heading northeast from Georgia.

During the day, the weather changed.

Before closing the office Saturday evening, Dunn reviewed the latest reports from Washington. Meteorologists now predicted the Midwest snowstorm would die out before it reached New York. The southern front, they thought, would blow out into the Atlantic Ocean once it reached North Carolina.

Dunn telegraphed this forecast to the area newspapers: Sunday will be colder, partly cloudy with brisk winds, followed by clear conditions.

As he turned off the office lights, Dunn spotted the Brooklyn Bridge through the window. Stars lit up the nation's first steel-wire suspension bridge.

The Brooklyn Bridge

Spanning the East River, this marvel of technology symbolized New York's greatness. Nothing could stop the city's progress. Dunn locked up and went home.

For the next 19 hours, no one would be overseeing the changing weather. Old Man Winter chuckled and went to work.

———— ◆ ————

First, Old Man Winter blew cold Canadian air down the East Coast. Then, when the southern storm left North Carolina's coast, he forced it north instead of blowing it out to sea. When this warm southern wind swallowed the icy Canadian breeze, it twisted and flipped. The skies roiled and the sea churned.

Next, Old Man Winter swatted the Midwest storm on its snowy behind, sending snow-filled clouds hurtling over the Appalachian Mountains toward the Northeast.

The two storm fronts met in Lewes, Delaware, and it was not a friendly encounter. This small town is located halfway between Florida and New England. It was a convenient stop for ship captains because the harbor was protected by a man-made breakwater.

On Sunday, March 11, a light rain fell from gloomy skies and the sea was restless. So were sailors onboard the 50 or so ships and small boats anchored inside the breakwater.

Great White Hurricane

The breakwater's wall of rock extended into the ocean, providing some shelter from the gusty winds blowing from the southeast. As night fell, the rain turned from a drizzle to a downpour.

Around midnight, Old Man Winter cranked the wind in the opposite direction. Southeasterly gusts changed into gale-force winds from the northwest.

"To the pier! To the pier!" people shouted, their voices shattering the night.

Townsfolk ran to the long wooden pier. Lanterns bobbed wildly in the rain, their light flickering across the ships crashing in the harbor. Waves dashed against the sides of the vessels, shredding their sails and slamming them into each other.

Timbers snapped in half. Anchors broke. Rudders froze. One tugboat rammed into the pier. Another collided with a steamship, sinking both vessels. Sailors climbed the rigging, trying to escape the waves' icy fingers.

Suddenly, the pier broke in three places, marooning some men on the far end with no way to span the 500 yards to shore. Soaked to the skin, the men stood as still as ice sculptures, afraid the slightest movement would cause the pier to collapse into the surf.

Rescue efforts took hours.

Finally, around dusk on Monday, March 12, professionals from a lifesaving station fired a harpoon gun at the marooned men. A rope fixed to the gun was also attached to a light boat, which the men managed to pull in and board, escaping before the pier sunk.

That day, 40 people were rescued from the Lewes Harbor. Three bodies washed ashore and 35 vessels were destroyed.

———◆———

As men fought the surf in Lewes, New Yorkers were dodging the rain on Sunday. This was no spring drizzle, but a pin-pricking downpour. As the day wore on, temperatures plunged and the wet streets and sidewalks turned to ice.

That evening, the weather service office reopened. Dunn was curious about what the office in Washington had to say. This was certainly not the partly cloudy day the experts had predicted.

There was no word from Washington. The telegraph lines were down.

While Dunn was trying to contact Washington, Sara Wilson was boarding a train in Buffalo. She was headed to Albany, New York, on her first trip away from home. She wore her new, red-feathered hat for the occasion.

Great White Hurricane

The conductor told the passengers they would reach their destination ahead of schedule.

Almost immediately after leaving Buffalo, rain began to pummel the train windows. Powerful wind gusts pushed the wooden train cars side to side. Despite the rocky movement, Wilson fell asleep.

When she woke, the rain had turned to thick, heavy snow. The train, now hours behind schedule, crawled along the track, which was covered in places by huge drifts. Two miles out of Albany, the train came upon a gigantic drift. Without warning the passengers, the engineer decided to plow through it.

The snow wall was as solid as concrete. When the train hit, the impact hurled passengers and luggage into the aisles. The iron stoves used to heat the cars toppled over, spilling coals on the carpet. Flames scampered up the window curtains and in minutes, the cars were on fire.

Everyone had to get off the train or burn to death.

Sara Wilson put on her hat and followed the other passengers into the snowstorm. Train officials told the passengers to divide into groups of four and walk to Albany, only 2 miles away.

People had dressed for a comfortable train ride, not a blizzard! Snow filled Wilson's shoes and the wind slipped under her skirt and down her sleeves.

Her new hat did not keep the frost from biting her ears. Her lashes froze until she could barely see the men ahead of her.

Wilson became tired and lagged behind the others. Shorter and weaker than the men in her group, she could not plow through the high drifts. She got stuck in a waist-high drift and the men pulled her out, but Wilson was too tired to walk any further.

The men in her group took turns carrying her, but soon they tired, too. The snow was too deep and the wind too strong.

You must carry on, the men told her. They set her down and urged her to walk.

Wilson tried, but in minutes, the men had vanished and she was alone in the storm. She decided to rest for a while. Sara sat down, gripping her hat tightly in her hand so the wind would not snatch it away. The hat's feather was brilliant red against the white snow.

❖

Sam Strong woke up Monday morning as usual and got ready for school. His aunt was expecting a dressmaker to come that day and she needed a corset needle. Would Sam run to the nearby shop to pick one up before going to school?

Sam glanced out the window. "It's snowing!"

His aunt helped Sam suit up. He put on high rubber boots, a heavy coat, and a woolen cap, gloves, and scarf.

"There," his aunt said. "You could go to the North Pole in that outfit. Now, hurry so you won't be late for school."

Sam opened the front door to find the steps buried under the snow. He slid down to where the sidewalk should have been. At first, as Sam plowed through the snow, the quest to find a corset needle was an adventure. The streets were practically empty and the snow was beautiful.

Then, a gust of wind picked Sam up and dumped him in a gigantic snow drift. A passing police officer hauled the boy out and told him to go home. But Sam did not want to disappoint his aunt, so he trudged on.

With his head down, cap pulled low, and scarf pulled high, only Sam's eyes were visible. Wagons and carriages sat abandoned on the street, and only one lonely street car struggled along.

Phone and telegraph wires, as well as cables for streetcars and the elevated trains, all hung from poles above ground. Covered in snow and ice, a forest of broken poles fell across streets and sidewalks, their lines a tangled mess.

Walking took every ounce of Sam's strength, but he finally reached the shop, only to find it closed. Its door and windows were covered in snow drifts. However, Sam Strong was not a quitter. He walked another half mile looking for an open shop, but the city was deserted. Finally, he ran into another pedestrian.

Shouting to be heard over the howling wind, Sam asked if the man knew where "a corset needle could be bought."

The man looked at Sam as though he had to be kidding. The stranger's reply taught Sam "a few new and attractive . . . expressions to add to my vocabulary of cuss words," he later said. The man ordered Sam to go home.

This time, the boy obeyed.

Four hours after he had left, Sam returned home. He clawed his way up the snow-covered front stoop and his panicked aunt and uncle hauled him into the house.

Although the dressmaker had never shown up and Sam's aunt apologized for sending him into such a storm, the boy cried. He had failed in his quest. His aunt rubbed the circulation back into Sam's icy body, gave him a slug of whiskey, and put him to bed. Sam slept the rest of the day.

———◆———

Great White Hurricane

photo credit: Library of Congress

Sam Strong was not the only New Yorker trying to get somewhere on Monday. In 1888, workers had few legal rights. They could get fired for not showing up to work.

So, people headed into the blizzard.

As 6 a.m., the temperature was only 23 degrees Fahrenheit (-5 degrees Celsius) and falling. Winds blew at 36 miles per hour, but gusts were reaching 84 miles an hour. The wind tossed signs, hats, newspapers, and umbrellas through the air. Frozen sparrows dropped from the sky.

Shoveling was useless because the wind blew the snow right back onto the sidewalks. People described the snow as painful, like the "lashes of a whip" or "flying glass."

Chauncey Depew, the president of the New York Central Railroad, reached Grand Central Depot Monday morning and immediately knew he had a problem. Grand Central should have been full of trains coming from outside New York—passenger trains, mail trains, trains with coal and food and other goods.

But the depot was empty. That meant trains were stalled on the tracks. With all communication down, Depew did not know where the trouble was.

The backup was at a section of track the railroad workers called the "Spike." Near the top of Manhattan Island, the Hudson River meets the Spuyten Duyvil Creek. Here, the railroad makes a 500-foot curve.

A 150-foot-high cliff looms on one side of the track and the Hudson River winds along the other side. If a train had to stop in the middle of the Spike, train engineers coming toward or behind the train wouldn't be able to see it.

At 6:40 a.m. on Monday, a commuter train hit a huge drift at the north end of the Spike and got stuck. Minutes later, another commuter train came around the curve and plowed into the first train.

Before long, eight trains were stalled on the Spike, their line of cars stretching a mile long.

Samuel Davis, a telegraph operator on the first train, lived nearby. He made it home and told his wife and mother to make bread and coffee. Then, Davis went to a nearby grocery store and bought sandwich fixings.

During the next three days, the Davis women made 300 sandwiches and huge kettles of coffee. The 100 passengers on the eight stalled trains had to share the only six mugs on the trains, but no one complained. They were alive and fed, which was better than passengers elsewhere in the city.

One by one, New York's four elevated trains ground to a halt on the ice-covered tracks. This left 15,000 passengers stranded on trestles above the city. As the hours passed, some people went stir-crazy. Resourceful men found ladders and charged people $2 each to climb down to the streets below.

Most passengers stayed put, afraid of falling from the icy trestles.

The situation was dangerous. When an elevated train on the Third Avenue line rammed into a train that was stalled on a hill, an engineer was crushed and 14 passengers were injured.

Horse-drawn streetcars were no better than steam locomotives. The snow was too deep and the streets too icy for the poor horses. Some animals dropped dead from exhaustion.

Drivers realized the toll the storm was taking on their horses. So they unhitched the animals, abandoning the streetcars and their passengers in the middle of the street.

Ferries that linked Manhattan to New Jersey, Long Island, and Staten Island stopped running when the rivers filled with ice floes. Officials closed down the Brooklyn Bridge because they did not know what such a storm might do to a suspension bridge. The innovative architecture was only five years old and hadn't been tested yet in severe weather conditions such as these.

Old Man Winter even managed to stop New York's economy. Only 30 stockbrokers showed up to the Wall Street Stock Exchange, so officials shut it down. The city's 70 banks received only a fraction of their usual deposits, so cashiers refused to guarantee checks written that day. No judges or juries showed up to the courthouse, so trials were canceled.

The only businesses that did well during the blizzard were saloons and hotels. Taverns offered refreshment and company. Before dusk on Monday, most hotels were filled to capacity. Some even rented out their chairs and closets.

Smith McNell's Hotel had only 420 rooms and it sheltered 800 people. One wealthy woman who was a frequent guest at the ritzy Astor Hotel was forced to sleep in a bathtub because no other space was available.

Poor people suffered the worst. Many low-income New Yorkers lived in crowded tenement apartments. Four families might share the one sink located in the hall. The only toilets were found outside in the outhouses, but these could not be reached during the blizzard.

People ran out of food, surviving on dry bread, cheese, and a little cabbage. Residents ran out of coal, so they dressed in layers and burned furniture to keep warm.

New York's 60,000 homeless had it even worse. Lucky ones found refuge in one of the city's 25 private shelters. Some found space in a church. Others rented floor space in private cellars for three cents a night.

So many homeless people turned themselves in as vagrants that the city's jail cells overflowed. At this time, it was a crime to be a homeless beggar. A jail clerk offered to forgive the crime and set everyone free, but the people said no thanks. Better a night in a jail than a night in Old Man Winter's chilly arms.

◆

On Monday night, the storm headed for Massachusetts. But before the people of New York could even begin to dig themselves out, Old Man Winter turned the storm back around for another shot at New York City.

People woke on Tuesday, March 13, to a white hurricane.

At this time in history, clearing snow from the streets was not considered the government's job. But New York's superintendent of streets, Jacob Coleman, wanted the snow shoveled so police and fire crews could get where they were needed. He estimated that below 42nd Street, roughly 3½ million cubic yards of snow had to be removed. This would require laborers to haul 12 million cartloads of snow to the piers to dump it in the rivers.

Shovels, carts, and workers were in high demand, so prices skyrocketed. The city and the railroad hired thousands of Italian immigrants to shovel out the streets and trains.

Young boys saw an opportunity to make a buck. Armed with brooms, shovels, and ice picks, these kids cleaned stoops and sidewalks. Some of them earned as much as $25 that day, which was good money for 1888.

Great White Hurricane

Commuters showed up for ferries on Tuesday, hoping to reach their jobs or homes. But the ferries could not cross the East River.

The river was a saltwater channel and never froze solid. But overnight a huge ice floe from the Hudson River had floated on the rising tide into the bay and entered the East River. The 6-inch-thick island of ice became wedged under the Brooklyn Bridge, stuck between Brooklyn and Manhattan. City officials ordered tugboats into the river to break up the ice.

One of the men waiting for a ferry decided he could walk to Brooklyn.

He slid down a post and stepped onto the ice. When other people saw him skate his way to Brooklyn, they decided to try it. Dockworkers rigged up ladders and charged a nickel for people who wanted to climb down. Hordes of young boys simply slid down the posts. Soon, 3,000 people were gliding on the East River.

By mid-morning, the ice began to grumble as the tide shifted. Police ordered people off the ice, but not everyone obeyed.

With loud creaks and groans, the ice floe broke up, stranding people who had not left the ice soon enough. One chunk began to float out to sea carrying 50 people on top of it! As the ice cake passed the Fulton Ferry Pier, some of the trapped men tried

photo credit: British Library

to grab hold of the pilings, but the posts were too
slippery. One man fell to his knees and prayed.
Another man shouted that he would send a cable
when he reached Europe.

As tugboats headed out to rescue the marooned
daredevils, their ice cake collided with another pier
and became stuck. Dockworkers lowered ladders and
ropes and pulled the people up to safety.

◆

By Wednesday, Old Man Winter decided New York
City had been taught its lesson. A timid sun showed

her face that afternoon, the snow stopped, and the temperature rose to 39 degrees Fahrenheit (4 degrees Celsius).

New Yorkers were relieved enough to find humor in their situation.

A florist filled his snowdrift with unsold flowers and a sign that said "Don't Pick the Flowers." A roofer put a sign on the drift that reached the top of his roof. The sign stated, "Now is the Time to Paint your Roof."

Others signs advertised "snow for sale," and "It's Snow Joke," and "Do you get my drift?" Two young boys dug a 75-foot path through the drifts that led people to a dead end.

This lightheartedness helped people take their minds off the tragedy around them. City residents were running out of coal and food. Trains were still snowbound as the railroad tracks remained buried in drifts. Digging the city out had become a matter of life and death.

The 17,000 laborers hired by the city worked double time.

Chauncey Depew sent sleighs to rescue people from stalled trains as crews continued to dig through the drifts and remove downed utility poles. Most trains were dug out by Wednesday. Food and coal began to trickle into the city and no one starved to death.

Sara Wilson, the girl in the red hat, never reached her destination. On Tuesday afternoon, officials compiled a list of passengers who had been on the burned train from Buffalo.

Someone remembered that a pretty, young girl had been on the train.

Searchers traced the route from the train wreckage and discovered Wilson's frozen body. The girl still clutched her new hat with its scarlet feather.

Sara Wilson was not the only person killed by Old Man Winter in the Great Blizzard of '88. An estimated 400 people died on land and another 100 died at sea. In addition, the storm cost New York City $20 million in property damage and half a million in lost wages.

On Wednesday, Sergeant Dunn's forecast predicted "fair and increasingly warm weather." New Yorkers hoped the forecast was accurate this time.

By Thursday, the sounds of the city had returned. Bells on horse-drawn vehicles clanged and locomotives chuffed. Newspaper boys cried out the headlines and street peddlers hawked their wares. Steamboats on the river blasted their horns and the fingers of telegraph operators clicked and clacked.

As the weather warmed and New York returned to life, Old Man Winter packed it in for the year. But some snowdrifts of the Great Blizzard of '88 lingered until the end of June.

Great White Hurricane

These were just Old Man Winter's way of letting people know—he would return.

New York City learned an important lesson in 1888, a lesson that remains in cities today. Prior to the storm, a law required companies to bury telephone and telegraph wires underground and remove utility poles. However, the government never enforced the law because powerful people in the communication companies opposed it.

After the blizzard, companies that did not obey the law were fined. By 1894, all wires in New York City were buried underground. Other cities followed New York's example.

The superstorm also convinced people that elevated railways were too vulnerable to bad weather. By 1904, an underground subway carried half a million New Yorkers around the city no matter the weather aboveground.

Politicians also learned a lesson. New York Mayor Abram Hewitt was not reelected in November 1888, partly because people blamed him for the chaos caused by the blizzard. Leaders realized their job security depended on how well they handled emergencies. New York and other cities developed disaster preparation plans and hired permanent workers to remove trash and snow.

NEW YORK

●
ERIE

PENNSYLVANIA

●
WILLIAMSPORT

SOUTH FORK
RESERVOIR
SOUTH FORK
HUNTING AND
FISHING CLUB

●
HARRISBURG

●
PITTSBURGH

MARYLAND

WEST
VIRGINIA

May 1889.
A dam holding a lake
atop a mountain where
wealthy people enjoy
themselves bursts open
during a great rainstorm.
The wall of water
released causes death and
destruction in the town
of Johnstown, below.

YOU
ARE
HERE

N
W E
S

Chapter Three

Wall of Water

This is a story about a kingdom on a mountain and the valley folk below. On the mountain, rich people played. Down in the valley, common people worked. The rich built a lake, deep and wide and mighty, for their own pleasure. A dam kept the water in the lake away from the valley people.

But one day, it began to rain. And rain and rain and rain.

The lake swelled, growing bigger and stronger and more insistent. It pounded on the walls of the dam, demanding to be released. And then one day, the dam stepped aside. The lake raced down the mountain and swallowed the valley whole.

A few valley people managed to survive. They rose up in anger against the mountain people for allowing the lake to escape. But alas, the kingdom of the rich proved as hard to defeat as the waters of the lake.

This is no fairy tale, but the true story of the most deadly dam failure in American history. It happened in Johnstown, Pennsylvania, on May 31, 1889.

◆

In the foothills of the Allegheny Mountains, Johnstown sat between Little Conemaugh River and Stony Creek River. The 30,000 residents of this valley were hardworking people. The lifeblood of the city was the Cambria Iron Company. This iron mill produced steel for railroads, barbed wire, farm plows, and other metal products needed by the growing nation. Cambria's furnaces glowed so red at night, the valley looked like it was on fire.

Men made about $10 a week for working 12 hours a day, Monday through Saturday. They rented cheap company houses along the riverbanks. One local man recalled, "People were poor, very poor by later standards, but they didn't know it."

Johnstown was an industrial city, full of smoke, ash, and dirt, but it was surrounded by beauty. The foothills of the Alleghenies swelled like the waves of a green sea in every direction.

In the thickly wooded ridges above the town, the stench of the iron mill vanished. The air was clear and sweet. Black bear and wildcats roamed the hills. Eagles, pheasants, geese, and loons were plentiful. Scores of little creeks and streams flowed into Stony Creek River and Little Conemaugh River.

Johnstown was built on a flood plain, and residents were used to water in the streets in spring. Small floods were a fact of life.

Victor Heiser, 16 years old, was one of the valley people. His parents, George and Mathilde, owned a store on Washington Street. The family lived above it. Victor's dream was to build a raft and float down the Conemaugh River until he reached the mighty Mississippi. During the summer, Victor liked to explore the land above the valley. When he heard about the kingdom with sailboats on the mountain, he just had to see it for himself.

---◆---

The official name of the mountain kingdom was the South Fork Hunting and Fishing Club. It was the property of some of the richest and most powerful men in the United States.

The late nineteenth century was an age when money talked, and these financiers and industrialists had lots of it.

Few laws restricted what these business owners could do to their workers, their competitors, their consumers, or the environment. Men with last names such as Frick, Carnegie, and Mellon clawed their way from rags to riches.

They earned the name "robber barons" because of their ruthless business practices and the huge influence they had over the government.

The robber barons who owned the South Fork Hunting and Fishing Club lived in Pittsburgh, Pennsylvania, about one hour from Johnstown. In this industrial heartland, these men owned coke-manufacturing companies, steel mills, glass factories, and coal mines. Their plants operated all day, every day, churning out what America needed to expand.

But these factories also spewed out smoke and smog and slime. The robber barons wanted to escape to someplace clean and beautiful. They found just such a place in South Fork.

Up the mountain above Johnstown, on a hill where the South Fork Creek flowed into Little Conemaugh River, perched the town of South Fork. The robber barons built their private club a couple miles from town.

When Victor Heiser came looking for sailboats in the sky, this is what he would have seen.

Wall of Water

A dusty road strolled from the village of South Fork, through the woods, arriving at the base of the South Fork Dam. The dam was the guardian of Lake Conemaugh. It loomed 72 feet above the valley floor and stretched more than 900 feet across. Grass and loose rocks covered its steep face, but as the dam aged, deep crevices formed, from which bushes and saplings grew.

To the east was the dam's spillway. This opening had been cut through the rock to release excess water from the lake so it would not spill over the dam's top and weaken the structure.

Victor would have followed the road to the right. After a short walk through the woods, he would have stepped into the sunshine on the top of the dam.

The view must have taken Victor's breath away.

Lake Conemaugh sat 7 feet below the top of the dam. In the spring of 1889, the lake covered 450 acres and was 70 feet deep in places. Fed by half a dozen creeks from the Blue Knob and Allegheny Mountains, the lake held 20 million tons of water.

Rowboats, canoes, two steam yachts, and even an electric catamaran dotted the lake. Most magnificently, in mountain country where trees and rocks crowded every stream, sailboats skimmed across the open water.

If Victor had looked over at the other side of the dam, he would have seen the abrupt drop off and the glint of the South Fork Creek where it flowed into the Little Conemaugh River. Johnstown, 14 miles downriver and behind several sharp turns, was not visible from the dam.

Following the road across the top of the dam for another mile, Victor would have reached the club's resort. The South Fork Hunting and Fishing Club not only owned the lake, dam, and 160 acres, but also 16 "cottages" and a clubhouse.

The cottages were mansions compared to Victor's apartment above the family store.

These multistory buildings had high ceilings, sweeping porches, and tinted glass windows. The clubhouse was luxurious with its massive stone fireplaces, billiard tables, fancy dining room, and 47 guest rooms. Across the spacious lawn, young women in long white dresses strolled on the arms of young men wearing suits and bowler hats.

By now, Victor would have been spotted by a groundskeeper and booted off the property. As a valley boy, he did not belong in the mountain kingdom.

———◆———

Wall of Water

The South Fork dam was not built to hold Lake Conemaugh. The dam was originally constructed by the state of Pennsylvania in 1852 to hold a 10-foot-deep reservoir for the state's canal system.

If built correctly, earthen dams are capable of holding back a lot of water. The South Fork dam was constructed of layers of clay, each coating made watertight before the next one was added.

The spillway cut into the rocky hillside on the eastern edge of the dam was key to the wall's strength. It prevented water from flowing over the dam's top, where it could seep inside the wall and erode the soil.

An essential safety feature was a set of sluice pipes in the center of the dam's base.

Five cast-iron pipes, 2 feet wide, were set into a stone culvert. These pipes were controlled by valves located in a nearby tower. When the pipes were closed, the reservoir filled with water. If the reservoir needed to be emptied in order to repair the dam or lowered if too much rain fell, the pipes could be opened, allowing water to drain into South Fork Creek.

The state abandoned its canal system when the railroad was built through Pennsylvania's mountains. In 1857, the Pennsylvania Railroad Company purchased the property around South Fork.

The dam came with the deal, but the railroad company had no use for it. For two decades, the dam was forgotten in the woods.

A congressman bought the property in 1875. The only change he made to the dam was to remove the cast iron sluice pipes and sell them as scrap metal. Then, in 1879, the Pittsburgh robber barons decided South Fork was the perfect spot to build a resort. All they needed was a lake.

The old dam could help them with that. They bought the dam and the 160 acres around it for $2,000.

Industrialist and real-estate developer Benjamin Ruff oversaw repairs to the dam. He filled the stone culvert with rock, mud, brush, and horse manure, but did not replace the sluice pipes. Ruff hired a man who had no engineering experience to repair the dam face.

Slowly, the basin behind the dam wall began to fill with spring water, and Lake Conemaugh was born.

In the summer of 1880, the robber barons stocked the lake. They ordered a special tank car from Lake Erie to transport 1,000 black bass at the cost of $1 per fish. That summer, families and friends of the robber barons arrived at South Fork. The era of the mountain kingdom had begun.

Wall of Water

◆

Some residents of Johnstown resented the people up on the mountain. The robber barons sent their message loud and clear: "No Trespassing" signs dotted trees and fence posts. Valley folk were not wanted there. But what concerned the valley people most was the safety of the dam.

The morning of June 10, 1881, a flash flood hit Johnstown. With the water came the rumor that the dam was about to burst. River floods were common, but now Lake Conemaugh loomed above Johnstown.

The dam did not break in 1881, but Daniel Johnson Morrell, the manager of the Cambria Iron Company, wanted proof that the dam was safe. He sent his own engineer, John Fulton, to investigate the structure.

Fulton's report, dated November 26, was not good news. He said repairs to the dam had not been done in "a careful . . . manner." Fulton claimed there were several problems with the dam, but the most worrisome was that there were no sluice pipes. Without these drainage pipes, the club could not control the water level in the lake.

Morrell forwarded the report to Benjamin Ruff, who dismissed Fulton's findings. In his reply to Morrell, Ruff wrote, "You and your people are in no danger."

But Morrell was not easily brushed off. He wrote to Ruff again on December 22, 1881. "We must protest against the erection of a dam at that place," Morrell stated, "that will be a perpetual menace to the lives and property of those residing in this . . . valley." He urged the club to make the needed repairs and even offered to help pay the cost.

Thanks, but no thanks, replied the robber barons.

Neither Fulton nor Morrell realized it, but the dam was even more dangerous than they thought, due to changes made by the club. In order to widen the road on the top of the dam so two carriages could easily pass each other, club owners lowered the dam wall by a couple feet.

To prevent fish from escaping through the spillway into South Fork Creek, the owners installed a screen over the spillway. This kept the fish in, but the screen became clogged with weeds and rocks. No lake water could pass through.

The dam also sagged in the middle at a spot where it had burst decades earlier when owned by the state. This sag made the dam's center 4 feet lower than its ends. When Fulton inspected the dam, the lake was only 40 feet deep, but the club eventually made Lake Conemaugh 65 feet deep.

The water reached almost to the top of this sag in the middle of the dam wall.

Perhaps Morrell would have fought the robber barons harder, but he was ill and died in 1885. Every spring, some valley residents predicted this would be the year the dam burst. But it never happened.

Townspeople became sick of false alarms. According to Victor, people believed the dam would give way someday, "but it won't ever happen to us."

Until it did.

Just after midnight on May 30, 1889, a major storm blew in from the Great Plains, dropping 8 inches of rain on western Pennsylvania in a few hours. Johnstown residents woke up to a dark and misty sky. The rivers were rising 1 foot per hour, and an avalanche of mud slammed into a brewery at dawn. Workers were sent home and schools closed.

The mist became a hard rain and the rivers flowed into streets and basements, 2 feet deep in some places and 10 feet in others. The Heisers' store was busy as people came in to buy supplies and talk about the weather. Some townsfolk moved their belongings to upper floors of their houses, while others waded through the water to seek shelter at the city's hotels.

Up on the mountain, the robber barons realized they had a problem.

Creeks running into the lake had become torrents, bringing not just water but also grass and brush and branches. The water was almost to the top of the dam and rising an inch per minute. John Parke, the club's 23-year-old engineer, said the lake made a "terrible roaring" sound.

In a desperate attempt to raise the top of the dam, a dozen men shoved and chopped at the road across its top. But even with all the rain, the road's dirt surface was packed tight. Other men tried to cut another spillway on the west side of the dam, but the rocky hillside was too tough.

As the water in the lake rose, so did the panic of club members at the scene. Several men tried to clear the debris clogging the fish screens in the spillway. But the rocks and branches were stuck tight. By 11 a.m., the outer face of the dam had sprung leaks.

It was time to warn the valley.

The message that the South Fork Dam was likely to break was carried by foot, phone, and telegraph to the villages dotting the mountainside. When the switchboard operator at the Western Union office in Johnstown received the message, she phoned the newspaper. The editor received the warning at 3:15.

But it was too late. By that time, Lake Conemaugh was already on its way down the mountain.

———◆———

Wall of Water

On the top of the mountain, club members and workers watched and waited. Lake water had gnawed a 10-foot-wide and 3-foot-deep hole in the outer face of the dam. At 3 in the afternoon, a hole "large enough to admit the passage of a train" broke through the dam.

The water ran through this gap for a few minutes and "then it just cut through like a knife." John Parke said the dam did not burst. Rather, "It simply moved away."

The time was 3:10 p.m.

Free from its earthen guardian at last, the lake leaped into the valley. Roaring as if going into battle, the water struck the treetops. The men on the mountain watched in horror as a bridge and farmhouse cartwheeled down the mountain before being hurled against a hillside and shattering.

Later studies proved the water poured out of its basin with the speed and depth of Niagara Falls, draining Lake Conemaugh in only 36 minutes. All that was left of the mountain kingdom's playground were acres of black ooze and flopping fish.

As it raced down the mountain, the lake water uprooted huge trees, yanked out fence posts, shoved over barns, and rolled boulders. Below South Fort, the water smashed into a 75-foot-tall stone aqueduct.

For a moment, the aqueduct held back the wall of water that was filled with timber, rock, and mud. The stone structure groaned with the effort. The lake water seethed and foamed, spitting up railroad ties, stumps, and planks. Behind the aqueduct, Lake Conemaugh reformed, 5½ miles from its original home. The lake waters gathered their collective strength and pushed. With a huge explosion, the aqueduct collapsed, water exploding down the mountain with even more force than before.

The little village of Mineral Point disappeared first. Then, the lake water plowed into the railroad yard at East Conemaugh, adding a dozen locomotives, passenger cars, houses, and corpses to its tidal wave.

Woodvale was next—the town of 1,000 people was gone in the blink of an eye.

———◆———

Victor was with his parents in the family quarters above the store. Although their barn was on higher ground than the house, Victor's father asked him to run to the barn and open the stalls in case the horses needed to swim.

Victor waded through 2 feet of water and pelting rain. He unlocked the stalls and was at the barn door, ready to dash back to the house.

Wall of Water

Suddenly, a tremendous roar filled the valley, quickly followed by several thunderous crashes.

Victor stood frozen at the barn door. He glanced up at the window where his parents stood. His father motioned frantically for Victor to climb up the trap door to the barn roof. Victory obeyed.

From atop the roof, Victor saw a wall move toward him with dizzying speed. It "was a dark mass in which seethed houses, freight cars, trees, and animals." The wall slammed into Washington Street. The Heiser store, with Victor's parents on the second floor, was "crushed like an eggshell" and disappeared.

In the next instant, the wall hit the barn. Unlike the store, the barn did not disintegrate. Instead, it stepped off its foundation and tumbled along the river that had been Washington Street only minutes earlier. Victor struggled to keep his balance as the barn headed straight for a neighbor's house. Just before the two buildings collided, Victor jumped.

He landed on the neighbor's roof, but the boards collapsed under his feet. Hanging desperately to the broken boards, Victor heaved himself out of the hole and scrambled monkey-like up the slippery roof.

Another house rolled past and Victor leaped again. This time his jump fell short.

Hands scrabbling for something solid, Victor gripped the eaves of the roof. As his body dangled above the roiling waters, the soaked shingles grew soft. Victor dug his fingernails into the wood, but the weight of his own body was too heavy.

He let go.

Miraculously, Victor landed back on the roof of his own barn. Dropping to his belly, he clung to the roof and rode the wildest water slide in history. Scenes of horror drifted past him.

The fruit dealer and his wife and children disappeared when a wave flipped over the wreckage they had been standing on. A neighbor lady rode astride a tar barrel, her body lurching as the bucking barrel tried to toss her. A servant stood stark naked on the roof of his master's house, hands raised as he prayed aloud. Everything and everyone was spinning toward a huge, arched stone bridge that spanned the Conemaugh River.

The wall of water was determined to get past the massive bridge. It shoved boxcars, factory roofs, telegraph poles, trees, barbed wire, houses, and dead livestock into the bridge's arches, creating another dam. Lake Conemaugh regrouped again, drowning more of the city.

Victor still lay on his barn roof. A back current shoved the barn roof behind a hill. The current was

photo credit: Ernest Walter Histed

slower there and Victor hopped onto the roof of a brick house that was still standing. Several other people were on the roof, too. From this shaky perch, the group managed to pull a few people to safety, but mostly they could only watch people drown.

As night fell, the rain continued to fall. Victor and the other miserable survivors huddled on the rooftop. They were so cold that they finally broke through a skylight and climbed into the house's attic. No one slept that night—they were kept awake by the groans of the house, the screams of the dying, and the roar of the lake waters.

The deadly flood became a deadly fire when the debris clogged against the stone bridge caught fire.

No one knows what caused the fire—perhaps coal spilled from stoves in the mangled houses or oil leaked from a derailed train engine. But that night, the mountain of debris went up in smoke with 80 people trapped inside.

In the last hour before dawn, the cries of the dying stopped and the roar of the water fell silent. Victor emerged from his attic refuge.

A smoky gray film hung over the valley, blurring the line between mountain and sky. The rain had finally stopped, and the lake waters were slowly slinking away as if ashamed of their destruction. Thousands of people gathered on the surrounding hillsides. Hundreds were injured, many were naked, and all were chilled to the bone.

Victor scrambled off the roof and waded to dry land. Then, he and the rest of Johnstown's survivors set off to search for missing loved ones. Thousands never found their families and friends.

After hunting for two weeks, Victor finally located his mother's corpse, but his father's remains were never identified.

Journalists flooded to the valley and reported the tragedy to the nation. Relief efforts began immediately.

Freight cars of food, clothing, and construction materials rolled as far as undamaged railroad tracks could carry them. These were followed by 1,000 volunteers, including undertakers and railroad workers. Clara Barton, the founder of the Red Cross, set up tent cities to shelter people until their homes could be rebuilt. Barton remained on the job for five months without taking a single day off.

The most urgent problem was identifying and burying the dead before bodies began to rot. Schoolhouses and saloons were turned into makeshift morgues where bodies were cleaned and numbered and identified when possible. More than 700 bodies that could not be identified were buried in a mass grave.

All in all, Lake Conemaugh killed 2,209 people, destroyed 1,600 homes, caused 17 million dollars of property damage, and flattened 4 square miles of Johnstown.

On Sunday, June 9, the sun broke through the clouds for the first time since the flood. On an embankment near the train depot, a preacher held an outdoor church service. After the prayers ended, John Fulton, the engineer who had examined South Fork Dam in 1881, rose to make an announcement.

Cambria Iron Company would be rebuilt. Fulton had taken over management of the iron mill after Daniel Morrell died.

"Get to work," he urged the crowd. "The furnaces are all right, the steel works are all right. Get to work, I say."

Everyone shouted, "Amen."

But Fulton was not finished. Since the dam broke, people had been muttering about whose fault it was. Fulton had someone to blame. He still had a copy of the report he had given to the South Fork Hunting and Fishing Club years ago.

"I told these people who . . . desired to seclude themselves in the mountains, that their dam was dangerous," Fulton said. The people of the valley vowed to hold the mountain kingdom responsible.

photo credit: Ron Shawley

Wall of Water

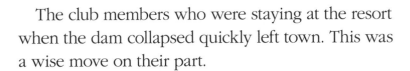

The club members who were staying at the resort when the dam collapsed quickly left town. This was a wise move on their part.

Three days after the disaster, an angry crowd of Johnstown men went up the mountain looking for heads to smash. They did not find any, so they smashed the resort's windows and furniture instead.

Many of the club members met in Pittsburgh to plan their next move. They decided to donate 1,000 blankets along with funds toward the relief effort. Andrew Carnegie donated the funds needed to rebuild the library.

This did not stop blame being heaped upon them from all sides, however.

Engineers investigated the cause of the flood. They faulted the club for not installing sluice pipes in the dam and for failing to repair the sag in the dam's center.

The American public was furious. How could such a disaster occur in the United States in 1889? Technology was advanced. The nation was prospering. Such tragedies seemed to belong to a bygone era.

The valley folk and other working class people like them latched on to one explanation of the disaster.

The robber barons had too much power.

These financiers and industrialists built their playground in the mountains at the expense of hardworking folks. When the South Fork dam broke, it not only opened a hole in the mountain, it also exposed the gap between America's superrich and everyone else.

Survivors filed lawsuits against the club and its members. Widows, orphans, people who had lost multiple family members and all their property—they wanted justice.

Sadly, they did not get it.

———◆———

The club members were some of the most powerful men in the country in the late nineteenth century. The nation's legal system had been supporting them for years. In 1886, the Pennsylvania Supreme Court had ruled that a mining company owned by one of the club members was not responsible for polluting a neighbor's land. "Personal inconveniences," the court wrote, "must yield to the necessities of a great public industry."

After the Johnstown flood, the court would stand behind the robber barons again. Club members hired top lawyers who argued the Johnstown flood was "an act of God."

In every lawsuit, the rulers of the mountain kingdom defeated the people of the valley.

However, change was in the wind. The public anger sparked by the Johnstown disaster pushed state governments to expand the power of the public to hold big businesses responsible for their actions. "Strict liability" became the new legal standard. Even if a company did not mean to be careless, it was still responsible for any damages it caused.

Only two years after Johnstown was destroyed by the South Fork dam, the Pennsylvania Supreme Court reversed its ruling in the 1886 case. The court found the Carnegie Company guilty of polluting its neighbor's land. "The production of iron or steel . . . [is] of great public importance," said the court, but the rights of the neighbor were equally important.

Meanwhile, Cambria Iron reopened and Johnstown slowly returned to life.

Victor Heiser had no desire to remain in the valley. The place was too haunted by memories of his parents. He worked his way through medical school, became an international public health doctor, and lived to be 100 years old.

The South Fork Hunting and Fishing Club was abandoned and the property sold. The robber barons never returned to their mountain kingdom.

OREGON

IDAHO

CALIFORNIA

NEVADA

UTAH

SAN
FRANCISCO

SAN ANDREAS FAULT

LOS
ANGELES

ARIZONA

PACIFIC
OCEAN

April 1906
A natural disaster joins
forces with incompetent
governing to spark
fires that rage unchecked
through the city of
San Francisco and kill
thousands of people.

YOU
ARE
HERE

N
W · E
S

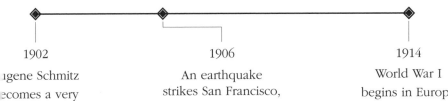

Chapter Four

Earth Dragon

Most of San Francisco was still asleep when the earth began to rumble. In the bedroom of his family's grocery store in Chinatown, 16-year-old Hugh Kwong Liang woke to his cousin's shouts.

"Get up! Get up!" Lung Tin yelled.

Hugh struggled to sit up, but his bed was rocking from side to side. Pictures jumped off the walls and a trunk slid across the floor. When Hugh understood what was happening, terror clutched his heart. The Earth Dragon had awakened, causing the earthquake of 1906.

San Francisco was the city where dreams came true. At least, people hoped this was so. Beginning in 1848, immigrants from all over the world flooded to California to find gold. By 1906, 450,000 people, most of them born outside of the United States, lived in San Francisco.

Hugh's father had left China in 1871. He moved to Chinatown, the 12-block neighborhood where Chinese immigrants lived. A lucky lottery ticket helped Hugh's father open up a grocery store. He married and had five children. Hugh was the oldest.

Chinese immigrants did not shed their culture when they settled in America. Chinese men wore their hair in "queues," or pigtails. Women dressed in black gowns over black pantaloons and wore sandals fitted over bound feet. This made them targets of racist whites.

When compared to the white residents of San Francisco, the Chinese looked different, spoke a different language, and practiced a different religion.

Racism flared when jobs were scarce. White people felt the "Pigtails" were taking their jobs. Newspaper editors fanned the flames by labeling the Chinese as dirty criminals who were "mentally inferior." Cries of "Yellow Peril" rang out up and down the West Coast. In 1882, the U.S. Congress responded by halting all Chinese immigration for 10 years.

Hugh grew up in this environment. Chinatown felt like an island of Chinese culture surrounded by a sea of hostile white people.

———◆———

San Francisco sits on a peninsula halfway up the California coast, with San Francisco Bay on one side and the Pacific Ocean on the other. In 1906, Market Street ran from the waterfront past hotels, office buildings, and shops, all the way to City Hall. Built only 10 years earlier, City Hall had a magnificent dome that was earthquake proof.

Or so people believed.

Despite its glossy surface, San Francisco had a dark underbelly. Criminals were free to break the law as long as they paid off the corrupt political machine that controlled the city. Attorney Abe Ruef was city boss, a man who wielded power behind the scenes. Ruef used blackmail and bribery to get his own candidate, Eugene Schmitz, elected mayor in 1901.

Ruef and Schmitz took bribes from everyone who did business in San Francisco. The telephone, telegraph, and transportation companies paid these politicians illegal fees for licenses to do business in the city. Anyone who wanted to construct a building, pave a road, or open a restaurant had to first pay Ruef and Schmitz.

This pair's corruption set the tone for the city. Criminal gangs bribed police to ignore opium dens in Chinatown and pickpockets on the waterfront.

Fire Chief Dennis Sullivan knew that the more money politicians took from the city treasury, the less there was to protect the city from fire. San Francisco had burned six previous times. In 1905, a report by an insurance group said the city needed major improvements or fire would eventually destroy it.

Buildings made of wood stood crowded together on narrow streets. Flames could easily jump from roof to roof across San Francisco.

San Francisco did not have enough pipes to distribute water in the event of a major fire. Nor did the city have enough water pressure in its fire hoses to reach flames in a tall building's upper floors.

For 13 years, Chief Sullivan worked to improve the fire department, but his funding requests clashed with the greed of politicians. When Sullivan learned that New York City had used dynamite to create firebreaks in 1835 to prevent a fire from destroying the city, he wanted his department to learn how to use this tool.

Army officials at the Presidio, the military base located outside the city, were willing to train firefighters to use dynamite safely. However, the army needed $1,000 to build a storage shed for the explosives.

Earth Dragon

San Francisco's harbor in the mid-1850s
photo credit: Library of Congress

San Francisco's Board of Supervisors, a group as corrupt as Mayor Schmitz, refused to provide funds.

Sullivan asked the city to build another water reservoir and to construct pumping stations to carry saltwater from the bay into the city in case of a big fire. The board refused these requests, too. Sullivan finally scheduled a meeting with a federal judge to force the city to improve fire safety. The meeting was scheduled for April 18, the day the Earth Dragon woke up.

———◆———

The planet's crust is like a jigsaw puzzle. The huge puzzle pieces are called tectonic plates. These plates fit together and only a powerful force can move them. The earth's core creates such a force.

The core at the center of the earth is as hot as the surface of the sun. This heat sends waves of pressure to the earth's crust. These waves push against the tectonic plates, creating cracks called faults.

San Francisco lies along the San Andreas Fault. This 10-mile-deep gash in California's bedrock stretches for 800 miles, ending north of San Francisco.

When the pressure inside the earth builds to a great intensity, it slides the plates that meet at the San Andreas Fault from side to side. The power released when these massive chunks of rock shift sends shock waves to the earth's surface. This is an earthquake.

Under the streets of San Francisco, the earth was beginning to move.

◆

Hugh Kwong Liang was too concerned with life above ground to consider the restless earth beneath his feet. Hugh lived like a prisoner in Chinatown. City officials refused to let the Chinese live outside Chinatown's borders, so 25,000 people lived crammed into a few blocks.

Hugh had ventured outside Chinatown a couple of times, but he had paid a price. White boys caught him by his queue and beat him up.

Occasionally, white people shopped at the Liang's store for delicacies such as eel, octopus, and shark fins. But Hugh overheard their rude whispers: "The Chinese are dirty. The Chinese eat rats."

Hugh's mother returned to China with Hugh's younger siblings in 1900. Nine-year-old Hugh remained with his father to tend the store. But five years later, Hugh's father died. A distant cousin, Lung Tin, moved in and took over the store. Life was hard, but at least Hugh had family.

Until the day the Earth Dragon awoke.

On April 18, 1906, at 5:12 a.m., 6 million tons of seismic energy dashed to the earth's surface at 7,000 miles an hour. The shock wave announced its arrival with a roar. Then, the ground under San Francisco buckled and shook.

Some buildings collapsed instantly. During the Gold Rush 50 years earlier, parts of the San Francisco Bay had been filled in with rotten timber, rocks, and loose earth to create more land for houses. When the quake shook this soft soil, it transformed into a dirt pudding, a process scientists call liquefaction.

Anything built on top of this pudding immediately fell to the ground.

Beds and pianos bounced up and down. Dishes jumped off shelves and portraits flew off walls. Sidewalks cracked and fences fell. Five hundred monuments in the Laurel Hill Cemetery tumbled. City Hall disintegrated until all that remained was its steel frame topped by the dome. The building looked a big, empty birdcage.

Less than a minute later, the shock wave ended. People tumbled out into the streets, wearing only half their clothes and stunned expressions. For a moment, there was an eerie silence.

Then panic set in.

Cries of pain and pleas for help escaped the wreckage of collapsed buildings. Rescuers dug through debris with their bare hands.

One trapped man was severely wounded and pleaded, "Shoot me! For God's sake, shoot me!" A police officer put the man out of his misery.

Along Market Street, a fisherman dashed into a huge refrigerator when the quake struck, pulling the door closed behind him. The foot-thick refrigerator walls saved him from being crushed, but then he was trapped inside the freezing cold box.

Hugh threw some items into a trunk that had belonged to his father, and he and Lung Tin ran from the store. Aftershocks still rippled through the earth, so no building was safe. They took refuge in Portsmouth Square, where the rest of Chinatown gathered, too.

Suddenly a bull came careening down the street. The animal had escaped from the stockyard when the earthquake hit. A shudder ran through the crowd. The Chinese believed the world was balanced on the backs of four bulls. No wonder the earth was tilting. This bull was supposed to be holding it up.

A police officer shot the terrified animal. But now, the Chinese feared the world would completely collapse without one of the bulls needed to hold it up. They swarmed into temples and scrawled prayers on red paper. These prayers were burned. Some ashes were tossed into the sky as an offering to the gods and others buried in the ground in an attempt to sooth the Earth Dragon.

The man the city would need most in the hours after the quake, Fire Chief Dennis Sullivan, was asleep in his apartment above the fire station when the earth cracked open. A chunk of stonework from the hotel next door crashed into the station roof, plowing through each floor and landing in the cellar.

Sullivan was unhurt, but when he went into the next room to help his wife, the floor collapsed under his feet.

The couple plummeted down into the cellar and was buried under debris. Sullivan landed next to a burst radiator that sprayed him with scalding water and steam.

Firefighters dug the chief out, and he was rushed to the hospital. Severely injured, Sullivan would not be able to lead his department in San Francisco's hour of greatest need.

The earthquake turned San Francisco into a giant pile of kindling waiting for a match. The shock wave knocked over chimneys and split gas mains. Seconds after the earthquake struck, at least 50 fires ignited around the city.

Engine Company No. 2. was the first fire station to answer an alarm. Firefighters climbed aboard horse-drawn fire engines. The station's Dalmatian raced ahead to bark out a warning at each intersection.

At the corner of Market and Kearney Streets, a building blazed. Smoke plumed from a crumbled chimney and flames crackled as they ate through the wreckage. The firefighters attached a hose to a hydrant and cranked the valve wide open.

No water came out.

They dragged their hose to a hydrant on another corner. That one was dry as well. So was every other hydrant nearby. Then word came that several more fires had ignited.

By 7 a.m., Engine Company No. 2 was surrounded by fire with no water to put it out.

The earthquake had ruptured more than 300 of the water pipes that snaked under the streets. About 80 million gallons of water sat in huge reservoirs outside the city, but there was no way to get it to the fires. Firefighters battled the blazes with shovels, axes, and their bare hands. They were no match for the strong winds that fanned every ember. Soon, fires blazed in almost every neighborhood.

With Chief Sullivan in the hospital, there was confusion about who should take charge of fighting the fires. In his absence, Mayor Schmitz and Brigadier General Frederick Funston of the Presidio both tried to take command.

Instead of saving the city, they helped destroy it.

Funston sent soldiers throughout the city to protect people and property. Many of these men worked tirelessly to aid terrified residents. Troops prodded exhausted people forward as they fled oncoming flames. Soldiers guarded the post office and U.S. Mint, where money was coined. They held people back from entering buildings close to collapse.

But while some soldiers offered help, others struck as much terror in people as the quake and fires did. One officer seized the bread of a grocer who had hiked prices. The officer tossed loaves to hungry people. The grocer insisted the bread was his property and he ordered the soldier to leave his store. The soldier took the grocer outside and shot him.

This was not an isolated incident.

The mayor ordered soldiers to destroy all liquor supplies in the city to prevent residents from getting drunk and rowdy, which would only add to the confusion and danger. The soldiers took the alcohol, but instead of destroying it, they drank it themselves. Then they were the drunk and rowdy ones.

Some soldiers stopped citizens from trying to douse fires that were destroying their own houses. At least one soldier clubbed people in the head with his rifle butt when they tried to help the exhausted firefighters.

When one man let his horse drink from a burst fire hose, a soldier shot the horse.

Then, an order from Mayor Schmitz gave the soldiers and the police a dangerous level of power. To maintain law and order, Schmitz ordered soldiers to shoot looters on sight. Anyone seen leaving a building with an armload of possessions was not questioned, arrested, or given a chance to defend himself.

He was immediately shot.

After the disaster ended, there were conflicting claims about how many so-called looters had been killed during the disaster. The army claimed only three men were shot. Eyewitness testimonies suggest the number could have been as high as 500.

Some of the worst looters were the soldiers themselves. As the fire approached a neighborhood, troops ordered residents to leave. Then, they entered the houses and took valuables. Soldiers stole guns from firearm stores, gloves from a glove factory, and diamonds from a jeweler. No one dared stop the soldiers because they carried the guns.

Throughout this chaos, the city continued to burn. By 2 p.m. on April 18, the chief operator at the main post office telegraphed to the rest of the nation, "The city practically ruined by fire. . . . Fire all around in every direction. . . . I want to get out of here or be blown up." Minutes later, the operator shut down. San Francisco was cut off from the world.

Years earlier, Fire Chief Sullivan had asked the city to train firefighters to use dynamite to create firebreaks. The Board of Supervisors had refused to fund the training. Now, with Sullivan in the hospital, Mayor Schmitz and General Funston decided dynamite was the only way to save the city. The mayor appointed firefighter John Dougherty as acting chief and approved his request to blow up certain buildings in order to deprive the fire of fuel.

The Presidio sent wagons of powdered and stick dynamite into the city, but neither the firefighters nor the soldiers on patrol knew how to use explosives to fight fire.

◆

The residents of Chinatown believed the gods had heard their prayers. The earth had stopped shaking and the fire was some distance away.

Hugh Kwong Liang sat in Portsmouth Square with his cousin. Smoke hung in the air, the odor of burning wood and charred flesh so strong Hugh could almost taste it. Thirst was as painful as a wound. The hours dragged on and the fires grew hotter, but there was little water available. At least Chinatown was safe, Hugh thought. Surely no flame could leap Portsmouth Square.

General Funston had other ideas. In order to create a firebreak, he ordered some buildings bordering Chinatown to be blown up. The soldiers were out of stick dynamite, so they used gunpowder, which was highly flammable and hard to control. Around 5 p.m., troops detonated a drugstore.

The building exploded, hurling a burning mattress across the street. This ignited a house on the edge of Chinatown. The winds picked up the flames, carrying them across Portsmouth Square.

In minutes, Chinatown was ablaze.

Years later, survivors remembered the sights and sounds of that day. The thud-thud-thud of countless trunks being pulled down cobblestone streets. Chinese women hobbling along on bound feet, children clasped to their chests. Men carrying long poles over their shoulders, bundles dangling from each end.

Hugh and Lung Tin tried to outrun the fire. Finally, Lung Tin stopped a man driving a wagon and bargained for a ride. The driver agreed to haul them for $50 each. Normally, such a ride cost $1.

Lung Tin handed the man $50 and turned to Hugh.

"I am sorry," he said. "I cannot take you with me. I do not have any more money."

Hugh was stunned. The store had been his father's. Hugh had worked there every day for years. His cousin had taken all the cash from the store before they fled. Surely, he had enough money for Hugh.

"You will survive," Lung Tin said. "You are young and an American citizen. Do not fear the future."

Lung Tin climbed into the cart. The driver flicked the reins and the horse moved off. Hugh stood alone, watching as the crowd swallowed up the last family he had in America.

Hugh finally broke down. "What is to become of me," he cried. "I am left penniless and all alone in this mess."

The fire forced Hugh to dry his tears. He grasped the handle of his father's trunk and followed the trail of refugees to the top of Nob Hill. There, he paused to catch his breath. Below him, all of Chinatown was on fire, and Hugh was overwhelmed with grief.

The Chinese stopped in a white neighborhood untouched by fire. Could they please take shelter? Doors were slammed in their faces.

Hugh reached the Presidio at 6 p.m. Soldiers distributed canvas tents—Hugh shared one with a teenage boy named Jimmy Ho. Jimmy had fled the fire empty-handed, so the only object in the tent was Hugh's trunk.

The boys were resting when a woman's piercing screams brought them to their feet. They ran to a nearby tent to find a young Chinese woman who had just given birth. Her husband was looking for a doctor.

Firebrands, or flaming embers, carried on the wind were gnawing through the canvas of the woman's tent and heating up the inside like an oven. Jimmy and Hugh put out the sparks and sprayed water on the tent's roof and walls. Then they returned to their own quarters, hoping to sleep.

Earth Dragon

When Hugh entered the tent, its emptiness was a blow to the stomach. While he and Jimmy were helping the woman, someone had entered the tent and stolen his father's trunk. It was the last connection Hugh had to his family.

A blanket of despair fell over Hugh. Jimmy tried to comfort him, but then told Hugh that he had to go search for relatives he believed were in the camp. Jimmy left and Hugh was alone again.

Night fell. The Presidio felt dangerous. Thieves lurked in this place, and Hugh wanted to escape from it. In fact, he wanted to escape from everything.

In a state of numbness, Hugh settled on a solution to his problems. He decided to kill himself. Hugh figured he had three options: Burn to death, starve to death, or drown. Leaving the Presidio behind, Hugh headed for the waterfront. He had decided to "jump into the water and drown. It was that simple."

◆

When the clock struck midnight on April 19, San Francisco looked like a war zone. Rubble filled the streets. Crushed and burned corpses lay untended. San Francisco's most valuable real estate—the financial district, theater district, shopping districts, and Chinatown—was in ashes.

Fortunately, the wharves at the end of Market Street were not damaged. The ferries and boats stationed there were the city's lifeline.

One of these became Hugh's lifeline, too.

After leaving the Presidio, Hugh walked aimlessly for hours. Finally, he saw a light flashing on the horizon. As he got closer, Hugh realized the light came from a boat. Two army trucks were parked along the waterfront and soldiers were loading supplies into the boat.

When the men were not looking, Hugh slipped onboard and hid under a table. Hugh vowed to jump overboard when the boat entered the deep part of the bay.

The thud of footsteps drew near and light flooded the room. Several men entered and began to talk about food. Hugh began to tremble—he tucked his arms and legs turtle-like under his body. What would the soldiers do if they found him, a Chinese boy, on their boat without permission?

"Look!" a man said. Suddenly, a hand clamped on Hugh's shoulder and dragged him out from under the table. Five men circled Hugh, angry scowls on their faces.

"What are you doing on my boat!" the captain demanded.

Hugh opened his mouth and the entire sad story poured out. The earthquake. His cousin's abandonment. The theft of his father's trunk. Hugh even confessed his plan to jump overboard.

To Hugh's surprise, the sailors' anger turned into pity. Sit down, they told him. Everything will be all right. Someone set a cup of coffee and a plate of food in front of him. Hugh realized he was starving. In the face of the crew's kindness, Hugh's despair felt lighter.

Maybe there was hope.

The next morning, the captain docked across the bay at Napa, California. The crew took up a collection and sent Hugh off with a pocketful of money and their best wishes. Hugh said these men were "the real Americans . . . a far cry from the race prejudice and discrimination that I knew." Hugh went off to find his future with hope restored.

While Hugh Kwong Liang embarked on his new life, San Francisco continued to burn. On April 19, fire chewed through churches and hotels, mansions and boarding houses, sparing neither rich nor poor.

However, the winds died down that night. The morning of Friday, April 20, the fire appeared to be just about burned out.

People were dancing with joy in the streets when the air split with a massive explosion.

The Viavi Company, a pharmaceutical warehouse, stood at the corner of Van Ness Avenue and Green Street. Unaware that thousands of gallons of alcohol were stored inside, the army dynamited the building. The flaming liquid shot into the air. Winds caught hold and blew the fire east.

The army's attempt to create a firebreak spawned another fire that destroyed 50 blocks.

In the predawn hours of the morning on Saturday, April 21, acting Fire Chief John Dougherty arrived at the Union Ferry for the last stand. The flames had to be stopped here or all the docks along the seawall would be destroyed and the city would be sealed off from the East Bay, trapping thousands.

In his mid-60s and only weeks from retirement, Dougherty drove his buggy to the frontline. He leaped out and grabbed a hose, thrusting it into a wall of fire.

Dougherty's men were awed by the old man's courage—they raced to help him. Hour after hour, the men battled the blazes. When someone collapsed in exhaustion, another firefighter pulled him to his feet and urged him to keep fighting. Helmets melted to heads. Jackets peeled off backs. Horses collapsed in their harnesses.

photo credit: Arnold Genthe

Yard by yard, the firemen forced the flames to retreat. By 7:15 a.m., the fire hissed and finally died. Buglers rode through the streets on horseback, crying, "The fire is out." The next day, it rained.

The government set up 26 camps around the city to house refugees in tents, barracks, and small cottages. Most Chinese refugees sought shelter across the bay in Oakland. The few hundred who stayed in San Francisco were booted out of one camp after another when white refugees complained about being housed with Chinese people.

Finally, city officials located the Chinese camp in a remote, cold, windy corner of the Presidio.

The embers of the fire were barely cool when Chinatown was looted. On April 27, white residents were allowed access to the city for the first time.

Many headed straight for Chinatown. The police arrested a handful of thieves, but no one was ever convicted.

Three days later, Chinese refugees were finally allowed back into Chinatown to see if anything was left of their former lives. But city officials had no intention of letting them rebuild their community.

For decades, white investors had wanted the valuable land on which Chinatown sat. Now, they saw an opportunity to relocate Chinatown outside San Francisco. But the normally meek Chinese mounted a fierce resistance. Chinese diplomats and leading Chinese businessmen presented a unified front when they met with city leaders.

The Chinese government owned the land on which the ruined Chinese embassy sat. The top diplomat told city leaders they had no legal right to take that land from China.

Merchants also chimed in. Chinatown had done $30 million worth of trade in 1905. Chinese property owners paid taxes to the city and Chinese renters paid rent to white landlords. If San Francisco did not want them, the Chinese would move to Portland or Seattle, places their money was wanted.

Then, without waiting for permission, merchants began to rebuild Chinatown with a new look: curved eaves, tiled roofs, incense-filled temples, and the chirp of fake crickets.

Earth Dragon

Tourists loved it. Chinatown brought visitors to San Francisco. Within two years, 15,000 Chinese had returned to the city.

Hugh Kwong Liang was not one of them. From Napa, he went to the city of Vallejo. There, he found an old family friend who took Hugh in, treating him like a son. Eventually, Hugh joined the first all-Chinese barbershop quartet. The group performed across California and even made it to Broadway.

Despite the catastrophe, Hugh found a new kind of family and managed to survive, even thrive.

The official death toll for the 1906 disaster was 498 people, a ridiculously low figure. City leaders used a fake number so people would not think San Francisco was a dangerous place to live or visit. A researcher who has studied the disaster in depth confirmed 3,000 deaths and believes the catastrophe actually killed between 5,000 and 10,000 people.

Improvements in building techniques have made earthquakes less destructive, but they are still unpredictable. Scientists do not know *when* another killer quake will strike San Francisco, but they are 100 percent certain one will. Sometime in the twenty-first century, the earth dragon will once again wake up and roar.

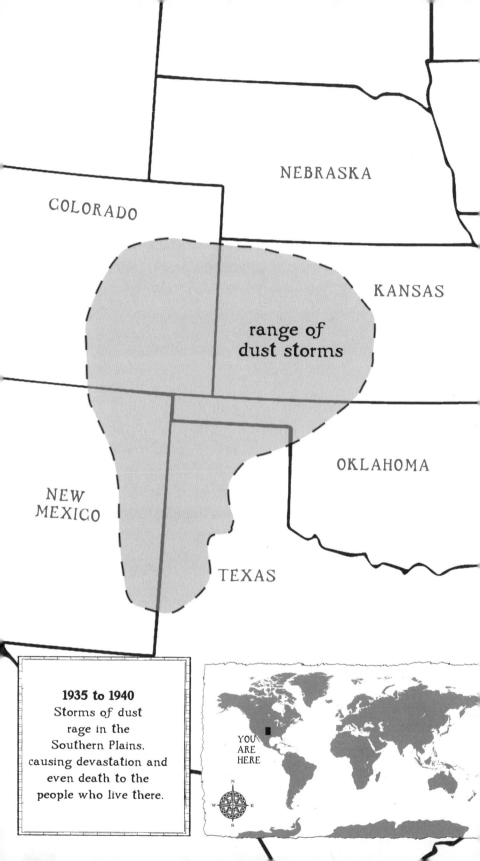

NEBRASKA

COLORADO

KANSAS

range of
dust storms

OKLAHOMA

NEW
MEXICO

TEXAS

1935 to 1940
Storms of dust
rage in the
Southern Plains,
causing devastation and
even death to the
people who live there.

YOU
ARE
HERE

Chapter Five
Black Sunday

The people of "No Man's Land" came to kill
jackrabbits. Tens of thousands of rabbits plagued
this section of the Oklahoma panhandle,
eating every last speck of vegetation that
the dust had not already killed. Farmers
could not take revenge on the sky that
refused to rain or the plants that refused
to grow, but they could kill jackrabbits.

The rabbit drive had been rescheduled several times
because of dust storms, but Sunday, April 14, 1935,
was a beautiful day. About 200 people, many of
them children, walked slowly across sand dunes and
around tumbleweeds, driving the rabbits toward the
fence, where men with clubs stood waiting.

As the killing began, someone yelled, "Look!"

The slaughter stopped and the crowd looked toward the horizon. A black tidal wave hurled through the air at 65 miles an hour. The mountain of dirt was 200 miles wide. As people ran for cover, the world turned black.

Black Sunday was one terrible day in a decade of terrible days for residents of the Dust Bowl. These Americans were victims of the nation's greatest man-made ecological disaster, one they had helped create.

———◆———

The Southern Plains expected humans to adapt to its environment, not the other way around. Native Americans figured out how to do this. First the Apache and then the Comanche thrived in this region, which included parts of Kansas, Colorado, Oklahoma, Texas, and New Mexico.

Native grasses covered this dry and treeless land, their roots deep enough to hold moisture even during the worst drought. The grass nurtured grouse and jackrabbits, deer and bison. Native Americans hunted the bison, using their flesh for food and their skin for clothing and shelter. The environment remained in balance.

Then, white people took over and tried to force the Southern Plains into something it was not.

Black Sunday

The army drove Native Americans onto reservations. White hunters slaughtered buffalo until only a few remained. Then, homesteaders moved in.

The Southern Plains had long been known as the "Great American Desert." The region receives less than 20 inches of rain per year. But, during the early twentieth century, the federal government wanted the land settled. It encouraged people to move there.

Farmers were told to practice dry farming. This meant planting wheat in the fall and letting it go dormant through the winter. In the spring, the short rainy season would grow the wheat, and then farmers could harvest it in early summer before the heat kicked in.

In 1908, the U.S. Congress passed the Enlarged Homestead Act. This law granted 320 acres of free land to anyone who cultivated the land for five years. Thousands of people relocated to No Man's Land, where they plowed up the grass and planted grain.

For several years, rain fell regularly. Scientists decided the climate had made a permanent shift.

The Great American Desert was now a breadbasket. Towns such as Boise City, Oklahoma, sprang up overnight.

World War I erupted in Europe in 1914. Suddenly, Americans wanted to buy American wheat instead of importing it from overseas.

A bushel of wheat sold for $2, good money in 1914. Hazel Lucas's family was one of many that moved to No Man's Land in 1914 to get their piece of the American dream.

◆

When the covered wagon stopped on the flat expanse of prairie, 10-year-old Hazel Lucas stood on the seat on her tippy toes to view her new home. Grass carpeted the flat land as far as she could see.

Carlie and Dee Lucas and their five children dug a hole in the side of the prairie south of Boise City. At first, Hazel Lucas hated living in a hole in the ground among the spiders and snakes. The stench of the dried cow dung they used as kindling burned her nostrils. She missed trees.

But soon, she fell in love with the prairie.

Life for the Lucas family improved with money from their wheat harvests. The family moved from the dugout into a wood-frame house and Hazel got a horse named Pecos. She played basketball for the Cimarron County High School girls' team, and when she was 16, Hazel met a boy named Charlie Shaw. Two years later, they married.

The more money the farmers made on wheat, the more wheat the farmers planted.

Banks were happy to issue loans for farmers to buy tractors and more land, so that's what farmers did—borrowed money and plowed land. The period of 1925 to 1930 was called the "Great Plow Up." More than 5,260,000 acres of Southern Plains were stripped of their natural grasses and planted in wheat.

Some farmers did not even live in No Man's Land. Called "suitcase farmers," these people planted wheat in the fall and then left, returning in late spring to harvest the crop. In 1919, more than 70 million acres of wheat were cultivated in the United States.

Some cowboys who had lived in the Southern Plains for decades warned against destroying the native sod. The rains could not last, they said. No Man's Land was only good for growing grass, they cautioned. But the farmers and government officials ignored the cowboys.

The Federal Bureau of Soils reported that America's soil was "the one resource that cannot be exhausted, that cannot be used up."

photo credit: U.S. Department of Agriculture

Earth, Wind, Fire, and Rain

Hazel and Charlie Shaw were not wheat farmers—they were teachers, a job that did not pay much. By the mid 1920s, farmers such as Shaw's dad discovered their wheat crops were not paying much either. When World War II ended in 1918, demand for American wheat began to fall. As demand fell, so did the price of wheat. By the end of the 1920s, the price of a bushel of wheat dropped to $1.50. Then it fell below a dollar, and then down to 75 cents.

To make the same amount of money they had a few years earlier, farmers needed to sell twice as much wheat. So, they planted more. In the summer of 1929, 50,000 acres of prairie grass were dug up each day. But nobody was buying the wheat.

Hazel Shaw's family was in trouble. She and Charlie moved to Cincinnati, Ohio, in 1929 so Charlie could attend school to become a mortician. Hazel's father, Carlie Lucas, died unexpectedly that spring. Only days before her mother and brothers were going to harvest the June wheat crop, a hailstorm struck. Grapefruit-sized hailstones crushed the wheat throughout No Man's Land. There would be no harvest.

Hazel did not have the money to help her family. She and her husband were so broke that she returned to Boise City in September to find a teaching job to pay their bills. She hoped next year would be better. Everyone in No Man's Land lived by this saying: *Next year will be better.*

The next year was not better. Not by a long shot.

On October 29, 1929, the stock market crashed. Billions of dollars of investors' money was lost as the value of companies' stock spiraled downward. Although most Americans did not own stock, the financial crisis still affected them.

Banks went bankrupt. Customers' savings disappeared overnight. Businesses laid off their workers and closed down. For the next 10 years, unemployment was high and wages were low. The 1930s was the decade of the Great Depression, the worst economic crisis in American history.

The school outside Boise City that hired Hazel could only pay her with a $10 I.O.U. that she was not able to cash in for a year. Farmers produced a bumper crop of wheat in 1930, but no one had the money to buy the grain.

As wheat rotted in grain elevators, hungry mobs rioted at a grocery store in Oklahoma City because they did not have enough money to buy bread.

Something was very wrong in America.

The government urged farmers to stop planting wheat, but farmers did the opposite. Desperate to sell enough to pay their debts, farmers dug up more grass and planted more grain. By the end of 1931, more than 30 million acres of the Southern Plains had been stripped of sod.

Then, the rains stopped. By 1932, drought baked the Southern Plains. The price of wheat was so low that it did not pay to plant a crop. Suitcase farmers abandoned their plots and farmers who lived in No Man's Land left their fields bare. The naked soil was at the mercy of the winds.

◆

At noon on January 21, 1932, a curtain of darkness fell over Amarillo, Texas. A cloud, 10,000 feet high, lurked on the edge of the city. Residents knew this was no rain cloud. And it didn't whirl like a twister. The cloud looked thick, as if it was made of fur. The strange force hovered for a while and then moved north toward Oklahoma.

As the dark mass entered No Man's Land, it left a trail of dust on the streets and tops of cars, across dining room tables, and inside peoples' nostrils.

People assumed the dirt cloud was a one-time freak of nature.

Black Sunday

But then, dust storms began to occur regularly. Locals called them "dusters." With the native grasses gone and the earth dry from the drought, brisk winds lifted the topsoil from No Man's Land and blew it in all directions. Entire fields rose into the sky, swirling and rolling in black blizzards.

One storm in April 1932 terrified Hazel's students. The sky turned black as night. Dirt slammed against the school's windows, shattering the glass. Children screamed as dirt poured into their classroom.

Drought and dusters transformed the land into an alien place where everything behaved strangely, even the bugs. Grasshoppers swarmed over the fields, munching anything green. Scores of centipedes crawled up curtains. Tarantulas appeared in bathtubs and black widows skittered across floors.

And jackrabbits were everywhere.

The people of No Man's Land could squash centipedes and shoot the jackrabbits, but they felt powerless against the dusters, which came more frequently and grew more powerful. In 1932, there were 14 dusters. In 1933, this number jumped to 38. One black blizzard lasted 24 hours.

The soil people had staked their futures on became an evil force. It broke windows and blinded cattle and filled peoples' lungs, turning into an illness doctors named "dust pneumonia."

One old timer said dusters were as dark as "two midnights in a jug."

Agricultural experts were baffled by what caused the dusters. Some people believed the Great American Desert had returned and farmers must leave the land because no one could survive there. But one man had a different explanation.

Hugh Hammond Bennett had grown up on a 1,200-acre plantation in North Carolina and had studied soil in college. After graduating, Bennett was hired to complete a soil survey in every state. While the Great Plow Up was underway, Bennett criticized the U.S. Department of Agriculture for declaring that soil was a resource that could not be used up.

Bennett believed farmers in the Southern Plains had plowed up too much grassland too quickly. With their tractors, farmers had changed the face of the earth more than volcanoes, earthquakes, tidal waves, and tornadoes combined.

Most scientists disagreed with Bennett. They believed dusters were due to weather, not farming methods. But in 1932, Franklin Delano Roosevelt was elected president. He promised to help all Americans suffering from the Great Depression, including the farmers.

President Roosevelt appointed Bennett to lead a new agency called the Soil Conservation Service.

A truck traveling in a dust storm
photo credit: Arthur Rothstein

Bennett worked with a team of soil experts to figure out strategies to keep the soil of the Southern Plains from taking flight. Meanwhile, the problems of No Man's Land got worse.

By 1934, dusters were a regular occurrence all year long. Storms were the strongest in southern Colorado, southwest Kansas, the panhandles of Texas and Oklahoma, and northeast New Mexico. At the center of this dusty circle was No Man's Land. Many farmers left the region, but Hazel and Charlie Shaw stayed. Charlie had finished his degree and opened up a funeral home in their house in Boise City.

Hazel was expecting a baby.

Everyone who chose to stay adapted to the changing environment. They lived in dust, ate dust, and breathed dust. Vaseline in their nostrils and masks over their faces did not stop soil particles from going up their noses and into their mouths. In the winter, snow fell as dark flakes that people called "snusters." The air was full of static electricity. Men stopped shaking hands because the shock was strong enough to knock a man off his feet.

Dirt got into everything.

In 1934, Shaw gave birth to a baby girl, Ruth Nell. Doctors suggested the Shaws might want to leave No Man's Land. The dust was full of silica. These rock fragments built up in the lungs and tore the air sacs, causing dust pneumonia. Children were more likely to develop it.

But Hazel Shaw's family had been one of the earliest homesteaders in the region. Her mother and siblings still lived in No Man's Land. Charlie Shaw's funeral home was just getting started. The Shaws decided to stay. Next year, things would get better.

The dusters did not get better in 1935—they got worse. In March, one storm blocked the sun for four days. Back roads to the homesteads were covered in sand dunes. The Red Cross warned people not to go outside unless absolutely necessary.

Little Ruth Nell Shaw coughed throughout the winter of 1935. Her mother taped around the doors and windows. She stuffed every crack with rags. Still, every morning, a scattering of oily, black dust appeared on Ruth Nell's crib and sometimes on her face. The doctor diagnosed the baby with whooping cough and advised the Shaws to leave.

Forty miles away from Boise City, Hazel Shaw's grandmother, Loumiza Lucas, was also coughing. The 80-year-old had stopped eating. She hated the dirt that ground between her teeth when she took a bite.

Two days before Ruth Nell's first birthday, Hazel Shaw and Ruth Nell took a train to Enid, Oklahoma, where Charlie Shaw's parents lived. The trip was slow because the train had to stop frequently so workers could shovel sand dunes off the tracks. Ruth Nell coughed so hard she broke one of her tiny ribs.

As soon as they reached Enid, Hazel rushed Ruth Nell to the hospital. The doctors diagnosed the child with dust pneumonia and gave her a crib in what they called the "dust ward." Ruth Nell developed a fever and refused to eat.

Shaw telephoned her husband. "You must come," she urged.

It took Charlie Shaw two days to drive 300 miles. He wore goggles and a face mask and had to hold his head out the window the entire time in order to see. The car veered off the road and tipped, but he righted it. The static electricity stalled the engine, but he got it restarted.

Finally, Charlie Shaw arrived in Enid and raced to the hospital. He ran into the dust ward, where he found his wife weeping. Ruth Nell had died an hour earlier. Back in No Man's Land, Loumiza Lucas slipped beneath her quilt and inhaled her last breath. She died only a few hours after her great-granddaughter.

The family decided to hold a double funeral for Ruth Nell and Loumiza in Boise City. The date for the ceremony was April 14, 1935.

◆

The morning of the funeral, the sunrise was pink and gold. The air smelled fresh and contained not a hint of dust. The wind had disappeared. People across No Man's Land emerged from their houses and looked around.

Naked trees. Scorched gardens. Hills and gullies of sand. It was a brown and barren land, but today the sun was shining. Maybe, just maybe, the better future the people had been praying for had finally arrived.

Rags were yanked from under doors. Windows were opened. Floors were scrubbed. Laundry was washed and hung on lines. Folks headed for the rabbit drive. On this fine day, they hoped to kill 50,000 jackrabbits.

But the Shaws faced a much sadder task that day.

Black Sunday

As the double funeral took place at St. Paul's Methodist Church in Boise City, hundreds of miles away the air over North Dakota turned violent. The winds screamed across the prairie at 100 miles per hour. Dust rose, reducing visibility to 300 feet. The soil entered South Dakota, then Nebraska, then it kept heading south.

At 3:00 in the afternoon, the funeral procession started for Texhoma, 40 miles away. Loumiza Lucas would be buried there next to her husband. Hazel and Charlie Shaw remained in Boise City with Ruth Nell's body. They planned to travel to Enid the next morning and bury their baby there. The Shaw's five-year-old niece, Carol, stayed behind with them. She played in the yard as Hazel and Charlie packed.

The funeral procession made very slow progress. The road was pockmarked with ruts and covered in drifts. Every car kicked up the dust. The mourners were only 6 miles out of Boise City when a shadow fell over the sun.

The wall of black was so tall and so wide it looked like a mountain range had suddenly appeared from nowhere.

The duster was at least 200 miles wide and racing toward them. Some people wanted to return to Boise City. Others thought that would be disrespectful to Grandma Loumiza. In minutes, there was no more time for discussion.

The cars drew close together. Everyone poured drinking water on their handkerchiefs, scarves, and shirts. They tied these garments over their faces.

Children crawled under the cars or on the floors of the cars. Adults lay flat on the ground, faces sheltered in their arms. Then, everything went black.

At the rabbit drive, people forgot about killing rabbits and scrambled to get inside their cars as the massive duster descended. One pickup truck full of teenagers made a dash for home but careened off the road into a ditch.

The teens draped a blanket over their heads, held hands, and walked blindly toward a schoolhouse they had seen earlier. They finally bumped into the building and crawled through an unlocked window. The temperature dropped and the wind blew. Dirt hammered against the walls, demanding to be let in.

The teenagers prayed that the world was not coming to an end.

Hazel Shaw was so full of grief she had not noticed the mountain of black roll toward Boise City. Suddenly, the sun vanished. She did not know where little Carol was.

Hazel stumbled around the house, calling for her niece. Every time she touched anything metal, a powerful shock ran through her body.

Black Sunday

Carol did not answer and Hazel panicked. She slammed into walls and knocked over dishes. Carol might have run the five blocks to her house, but the electricity from the duster had knocked out the telephones, so Hazel couldn't call her in-laws to ask.

Charlie Shaw grabbed a flashlight and went outside. The beam of light was instantly swallowed by the dark dirt. He called and called, but Carol did not answer. He dropped to his belly and slithered along the street, peeking under the cloud. Charlie Shaw crawled up to a door and banged on it, hoping it was the right house.

He had guessed correctly. Little Carol knew just what to do when a duster appeared in the sky. She had run home as soon as she saw the cloud and was safe and sound. Charlie Shaw refused to leave his wife alone during the black blizzard, so he slithered back home.

photo credit: NOAA George E. Marsh Album

The funeral procession with Grandma Loumiza's body finally reached Boise City around 10 p.m. Four men had walked hand in hand across the road, feeling the way with their feet, and slowly guided the mourners home.

A reporter named Robert Geiger happened to be in No Man's Land on Black Sunday and had sheltered in Boise City during the storm. The next day, he filed a story that coined a new term. "Three little words," Geiger wrote, "rule life today in the dust bowl of the continent—if it rains."

People did plan their future around those three words, "if it rains," but by 1935, many had given up on that dream. It was Geiger's other three words that summed up what life had become for them.

The Dust Bowl.

◆

Black Sunday was a turning point. For a few hours on the morning of April 14, 1935, people felt hopeful. They let themselves believe the environmental nightmare might be over. Then nature slammed reality back in their faces. Many decided they had had enough.

Despite the dangerous weather, the decision to leave No Man's Land was not easy for Hazel and Charlie Shaw.

Most of Hazel's family members were sticking it out. But in 1936, Hazel and Charlie had their second child, Charlie Jr. Hazel kept her son a prisoner in the house to protect him from dust.

The Dust Bowl was no place to raise a child.

At the end of 1936, the Shaws said goodbye to No Man's Land. The young girl who had stood on the seat of the covered wagon and gazed with excitement at the vast prairie now existed only in Hazel's memories. The Shaws moved to Vici, Oklahoma, out of the heart of the Dust Bowl.

As the decade labeled the "Dirty Thirties" neared its end, the federal government offered help to farmers willing to accept it. Farmers were paid 75 cents an acre to carry out wind erosion strategies. They knocked over dunes, plowed into the hard earth, and planted grass and feed crops to hold the soil in place.

When a duster came and destroyed everything, the farmers had to do the work all over again. The government also bought back millions of acres of farmland from people who just wanted to get out of No Man's Land.

Finally, in 1938, the rain returned.

But, as if nature wanted to give the Southern Plains one last kick, with the rain came a plague of grasshoppers. When the cloud appeared on the horizon, people prepared for another duster—but then they heard the buzzing.

The swarm was vast. One farmer counted the grasshoppers under one watermelon and used this figure to estimate how many of the insects landed on his farm. He calculated 23,400 grasshoppers per acre, or 14 million per square mile.

The grasshoppers devoured every bit of new plant growth. Their bodies crunched underfoot and turned the ground slick with blood and guts.

Farmers and government officials tried every means to kill the pests. They trapped the bugs in vats of kerosene. They poisoned them with a mixture of sawdust, molasses, and banana oil. They crushed them under tires.

When rain fell, every pond, river, and creek was black with grasshopper carcasses.

Despite the grasshopper invasion, the tide had turned. By 1939, regular rain and improvements in farming techniques shrunk the Dust Bowl to one-fifth of its previous size. In No Man's Land, flowers bloomed, cows grew plump, and there was enough grass to feed the jackrabbits so they stayed away from farmers' vegetable gardens.

Black Sunday

In 1940, the government declared an end to the decade-long drought. That year, farmers in the Southern Plains harvested their first profitable crop since 1930. World War II erupted in 1939, bringing prosperity to No Man's Land just as World War I had done 25 years earlier. Wheat prices skyrocketed. A crop that had brought in $1,000 in 1930 now sold for $12,000.

But history often repeats itself. From 1940 to 1945, farmers dug up another 3 million acres of the Great Plains and planted wheat. The suitcase farmers returned. Some farmers cancelled the soil erosion agreements they had signed with the Soil Conservation Service because they wanted to cultivate land.

During the 1950s, the drought returned and so did the dusters. But the "Filthy Fifties" were nowhere near as devastating as the Dirty Thirties. When the federal government purchased 4 million acres of land from farmers in the 1930s, it had planted native grass there. Even though some farmers cancelled their contracts with the Soil Conservation Service, many others embraced smart strategies to save their soil.

These people had learned the hard lesson of the Dust Bowl—if humans push too hard against nature, nature will push back.

Glossary

aftershock: an earthquake that happens after the initial shock.

agriculture: growing plants and raising animals for food and other products.

air pressure: the force of the air in the atmosphere pushing down on the earth.

aqueduct: a channel for moving water, usually in the form of a bridge over a valley.

architecture: the style or look of a building.

atmosphere: the blanket of gases around the earth.

atmospheric: relating to the atmosphere.

bankrupt: a business judged by a court as being unable to pay its debts.

barbershop quartet: a group of four singers, usually male, who sing without instrumentals in an old-fashioned style.

barter: to trade by exchanging one good or service for another.

bedrock: the solid rock underneath the earth's surface.

billiards: a game similar to pool in which three balls are struck with cue sticks into pockets around the table.

blackmail: an illegal act in which someone demands money from a person in return for not revealing information about that person that would be damaging.

blizzard: a severe snowstorm with high winds, low temperatures, and heavy snow.

boardinghouse: a house providing food and lodging for paying guests.

bound feet: the Chinese custom of applying a tight cloth binding to a young girl's feet in order to change their shape.

breadbasket: an area that produces grain for a larger area.

breakwater: a seawall or barrier built into a body of water to protect the shoreline from the force of the waves.

bribery: to give money or favors to someone in power so they will grant special treatment.

calamity: a disaster.

canal: a man-made waterway.

careen: to move swiftly in an uncontrolled manner.

catastrophe: something that is extremely harmful or damaging.

charred: partly burned with a blackened surface.

chemicals: substances that have certain features that can react with other substances.

cinder: a small piece of partly burned coal or wood that has stopped giving off flames but still has combustible matter in it.

city boss: a person who is not elected to public office but still controls a city's government from behind the scenes, often through illegal means.

civilization: a community of people that is advanced in art, science, and government.

coke: a solid fuel made by distilling coal.

combustible: something that can catch on fire and burn easily.

community: a group of people who live in the same place or who share key characteristics such as religion or language.

congregation: the people who regularly attend a church.

convection: the upward or downward movement of warm and cool air that forms many clouds.

convection column: the hot air around a flame that rises in a column of gas, smoke, and debris.

core: the center of an object.

corpse: a dead body.

corrupt: behaving dishonestly for money or personal gain.

corruption: the dishonest or illegal behavior of people in power.

corset: a woman's tightly fitted undergarment that runs from under the chest to the waist, which is meant to enhance her figure.

counterclockwise: the direction that goes opposite to the hands of a clock.

crevice: a narrow opening, especially in a rock or wall.

crisis: a time of great difficulty, trouble, or danger.

crop: a plant grown for food or other uses.

crust: the outer layer of the earth.

culture: the beliefs, customs, and practices of a society at a particular point in history.

culvert: a drain or pipe that runs under a road or railroad.

current: the steady flow of water or air in one direction.

dam: a strong barrier built across a stream or river to hold back water.

debris: the scattered pieces of something that has been broken or destroyed.

deposit: money put in a bank account.

detonate: to blow up.

devour: to eat hungrily and quickly.

diplomat: an official representing a country.

disintegrate: to break apart into small pieces.

distribute: to pass out or deliver something.

dormant: in a state of rest or inactivity.

douse: to drench with a liquid.

drought: a long period without rain that can often cause extensive damage to crops.

dune: a mound or ridge of sand that has been blown by the wind.

Dust Bowl: the area of the Great Plains where drought and soil erosion produced massive dust storms in the 1930s.

dust pneumonia: an illness caused by inhaling dust.

duster: a dust storm.

earthquake: a sudden movement in the outer layer of the earth. It releases stress built up from the motion of the earth's tectonic plates.

ebb: to retreat or go out.

ecological: having to do with the relationship between living things and their environment.

economy: the wealth and resources of a country or region.

elements: what the ancient Greeks believed were the basic building blocks of all life: earth, water, air, and fire.

embassy: the official residence of an ambassador, the top diplomat in a foreign country.

epic: grand or monumental.

erosion: wearing away of rock or soil by water and wind.

Eucharist: a Christian religious ceremony in which bread and wine are blessed and consumed.

fault: a crack in the earth's crust where tectonic plates move against each other.

fickle: changing often.

financier: a person who manages large amounts of money for a business.

firebreak: a strip of open space that can prevent the spread of fire.

flammable: easily burned.

floe: a sheet of floating ice.

flood plain: an area of low-lying ground susceptible to flooding.

foothill: a low hill at the base of mountains.

forecast: a prediction of the weather.

foundation: the base of a home that is partly underground.

front: the dividing point where two sides meet.

gangrene: the destruction of body tissue.

gore: bloody.

Great Depression: the severe slump in the economy during the 1930s, characterized by high unemployment and low wages.

gristmill: a mill for grinding grain.

grotesque: very weird.

havoc: widespread destruction.

homesteader: a person who is given land to farm by the government.

horizon: the line in the distance where the land or sea seems to meet the sky.

hydraulic: something operated by liquid moving in a confined space under pressure.

ignite: to catch fire.

ignorance: a lack of information or knowledge.

immigrant: a person who moves to a foreign country.

incinerate: to burn.

industrial: having to do with factories and manufacturing.

industrialist: a person who owns and manages a large factory.

inferior: lower in rank or status or quality.

inferno: a large, steadily burning fire.

inhalation: the action of breathing in.

innovative: coming up with new ideas or methods of doing things.

instability: not dependable or steady.

intact: not damaged.

investor: a person who puts money into a financial scheme with the expectation of making a profit from it.

justice: fair treatment under the law.

limelight: the center of public attention.

liquefaction: when an earthquake turns soil into liquid.

livestock: animals raised for food and other products.

looter: a person who steals goods during a time of crisis, such as a natural disaster.

low-pressure front: an area in the atmosphere where the air pressure is lighter than the air pressure around that area.

main: a pipe for distributing gas or water.

makeshift: a crude and temporary substitute.

maroon: to be isolated with little hope for escape.

menace: something or someone likely to cause harm.

meteorologist: a scientist who studies weather and makes predictions about it.

methane gas: a colorless, odorless, flammable gas.

miracle: an unusual or wonderful event believed to be caused by the power of God.

momentum: the force that a moving object has in the direction that it is moving.

morgue: a place where bodies are kept to be identified or claimed.

mortician: one whose business is to prepare the dead for burial and to arrange and manage funerals

natural disaster: a natural event, such as a fire or flood, that causes great damage.

No Man's Land: the northwest of the Texas panhandle and all of the Oklahoma panhandle.

nourishment: the food needed to survive.

opium: a reddish-brown, highly addictive drug.

panhandle: a narrow strip of land of one state that projects into another state.

pantaloons: baggy trousers gathered at the ankle.

paralyze: to prevent from moving.

parched: dried out.

peddler: a person who sells things, often on the street from carts or tables.

peninsula: a piece of land surrounded by water on three sides.

pew: a bench in a church.

pier: a structure built on posts that extends from land over the water. Used as a landing place for boats or for people to stroll on.

Glossary

piling: the posts that hold up any large structure, such as a pier or trestle.

Plains: a large, flat area of land in the middle of the country.

political machine: a political organization led by a city boss, usually a corrupt politician, who exchanges political favors for votes and bribes.

port: a place where ships can load and unload.

prairie: the wide, rolling land covered in grasses west of the Mississippi River.

prey: an animal hunted by a predator for food.

quench: to put out a fire or satisfy a thirst.

queue: the pigtail hairstyle worn by Chinese men.

racism: the belief that people of a different race than one's own are inferior.

ravenous: desperately hungry.

reform: to change something for the better.

refugee: a person forced to flee because of war, persecution, or a natural disaster.

reservoir: a large natural or artificial lake used as a water supply source.

resigned: giving up.

robber baron: a person who has become rich through ruthless business practices.

ruthless: willing to make other people suffer so that you can achieve your goals.

sacrament: a religious ceremony or act of the Christian church.

sacred: something valued because it is connected to people's religious beliefs.

saloon: a place to sell and drink alcohol.

salve: an ointment used to heal skin.

savior: the person or god-figure who saves people from physical or spiritual harm.

sawmill: a factory in which logs are sawed into lumber.

scald: to burn with a hot liquid or steam.

Scandinavia: the region of northern Europe that includes Norway, Sweden, Finland, and Denmark.

seawall: a wall or embankment built to prevent the sea from eroding the shoreline.

seismic: related to pressure in the earth's core and crust.

shock wave: a sharp change of pressure moving through the air caused by something moving faster than the speed of sound.

silica: a hard, colorless compound found in rocks.

sluice: a passage made for water to go through that is fitted with a valve or gate so the water level can be raised or lowered.

sod: the grass that covers the ground surface.

spigot: a faucet.

spillway: a passage for water to run over or around a dam.

Glossary

spontaneously: happening without an apparent cause.

stampede: a sudden uncontrolled rush of a group of people or animals.

stock: a share of ownership of a company.

stock exchange: a place where stocks are bought and sold.

stockbroker: someone who buys and sells stocks for a client.

strict liability: a legal standard that held a company responsible for damages it caused even when those damages were not intentional.

substation: a branch office associated with a main headquarters.

suffocate: to kill or destroy by cutting off access to air or oxygen.

supernatural: beings, objects, or events that cannot be explained.

suspension bridge: a bridge with a road suspended from cables attached to towers.

symbolize: to represent.

tabernacle: a container for the reserved sacrament of a Catholic church.

technology: the tools, methods, and systems used to solve a problem or do work.

tectonic plates: large slabs of the earth's crust that are in constant motion. The plates move on the hot, melted layer of earth below.

telegraph: a communication system that transmits electric impulses through wires, usually in Morse code.

tenement: a city apartment building that is of poor quality in terms of its sanitation, safety, and comfort.

tinderbox: something that can easily catch fire.

torrent: a rushing flood.

trestle: a framework of timber or steel for supporting a road or railroad over a gap.

undertaker: a mortician.

unemployment: joblessness.

unscathed: not harmed or injured.

urban: relating to cities.

vagrant: a homeless, jobless person.

visibility: the distance someone can see during certain weather conditions.

vulnerable: exposed to harm.

wharf: a structure built along the shore of a lake or ocean so ships can load and unload supplies and people.

woodenware: things made for the home out of wood, such as bowls and other dishes.

wrath: strong and vengeful anger.

Yellow Peril: a nineteenth-century phrase that expressed a fear that the United States was in danger from the growing power of China and Japan.

Resources

Books

Hesse, Karen. *Out of the Dust.* New York: Scholastic, 1997.

Knickelbine, Scott. *The Great Peshtigo Fire: Stories and Science from America's Deadliest Fire.* Madison, WI: Wisconsin Historical Society Press, 2012.

Murphy, Jim. *Blizzard! The Storm That Changed America.* New York: Scholastic, 2006.

Tarshis, Lauren. *I Survived Hurricane Katrina, 2005.* St. Louis, MO: Turtleback Books, 2011.

Yep, Laurence. *The Earth Dragon Awakes: The San Francisco Earthquake of 1906.* New York: HarperCollins, 2008.

Websites

Learn more about fire at NOVA's Fire Lab:
pbs.org/wgbh/nova/fire/onfi_text.html

Take a virtual tour of the Blizzard of 1888.
virtualny.ashp.cuny.edu/blizzard/bliz_hp.html

You can see a digital simulation of the Johnstown flood in this video.
youtube.com/watch?v=tMc9kP9q-d8

Dust storms aren't a thing of the past! Watch a recent one in this video.
youtube.com/watch?v=cYxm6jjy874

You can see photos of New Yorkers in the Blizzard of 1888.
mentalfloss.com/article/61301/photos-new-york -after-blizzard-1888

View the aftermath of the San Francisco fire and earthquake for yourself in this silent video.
loc.gov/item/00694425